Classic Cavs

CLASSIC CLEVELAND

Classic Browns: The 50 Greatest Games in Cleveland Browns History
JONATHAN KNIGHT

Classic Tribe: The 50 Greatest Games in Cleveland Indians History
JONATHAN KNIGHT

Classic Cavs: The 50 Greatest Games in Cleveland Cavaliers History
JONATHAN KNIGHT

Classic Cavs

THE 50 GREATEST GAMES IN CLEVELAND CAVALIERS HISTORY

Jonathan Knight

The Kent State University Press • Kent, Ohio

© 2009 by The Kent State University Press, Kent, Ohio 44242
All rights reserved.
Library of Congress Catalog Card Number 2009016515
ISBN 978-1-60635-011-9
Manufactured in the United States of America

Library of Congress Cataloging-in-Publication Data
Knight, Jonathan.
    Classic Cavs : the 50 greatest games in Cleveland Cavaliers history / by Jonathan Knight.
        p.   cm.
    ISBN 978-1-60635-011-9 (pbk. : alk. paper) ∞
    1. Cleveland Cavaliers (Basketball team). 2. Cleveland Cavaliers (Basketball team)—
History. 3. Basketball—History. I. Title. II. Title: 50 greatest games in Cleveland Cavaliers
history. III. Title: Fifty greatest games in Cleveland Cavaliers history.
    GV885.52.C57K65 2009
    796.323'640977132—dc22   2009016515

British Library Cataloging-in-Publication data are available.

13 12 11 10 09   5 4 3 2 1

To my mother for making our family special—and for keeping it together.

Contents

cavalier *(n.)—a gentleman trained in arms and horsemanship*
(adj.)—marked by or given to offhand and often
disdainful dismissal of important matters
—Merriam-Webster Dictionary

Preface

Ironically, my most vivid memory of a professional sports league, now represented by Web videos and constant television coverage, is of me lying flat on my stomach on a cold floor in a dark room with my head pressed against a stereo speaker trying to distinguish crowd noise from static. Or sometimes, the play-by-play action from a passing truck driver's late-night monologue or a neighbor's hair dryer.

By the late 1980s, the National Basketball Association had already emerged from its virtual anonymity outside New York, Boston, and Philadelphia, but it had yet to become the techno-thumping nightclub it would morph into as the century turned. To be sure, there were voluptuous dance teams and tremendous video screens in arenas back then, but scoreboards didn't spontaneously belch flames during pregame introductions and the between-action entertainment didn't resemble a rave portending the end of the world.

Cable television, guided into the NBA's waiting arms by Ted Turner minions TBS and TNT, was just beginning to tiptoe into the shallow end of live sports coverage, but an out-of-town fan could only count on catching his team in maybe three or four televised games per regular season. Nor could you flip on a computer and follow a game from start to finish (short of Nintendo's 8-bit classic Double Dribble). If you wanted to invest any interest in an NBA team beyond examining box scores in the morning paper, that left you with an electronic marvel that was essentially archaic even when "spam" was nothing more than gelatinous canned meat—radio.

For nearly five of my teen years, I followed the Cleveland Cavaliers with the passion of a well-financed junkie, and the radio was my dealer. There was, however, one final wrinkle to my predicament. Growing up outside of Dayton, Ohio, I was a good hundred miles from any of the Cavs' dozen or so affiliate stations. And even if I had been closer, the majority of them were tiny, hometown networks that would send out their signal upon wattage that wouldn't power a three-way lightbulb. My only option was to try to tune in to the horse's mouth itself—flagship station WWWE 1100 AM beaming out Cavs' action at 50,000 watts from Ohio's north coast.

It was right around this time I discovered, via a mind-numbing eighth-grade science class, that radio waves actually traveled better at night. And luckily for me, by the late twentieth century, 90 percent of all professional sporting events were played under cover of darkness. If the Cavs were playing on a Sunday afternoon, physics would shrug and tell me I was out of luck, but throughout the week, I could almost always pick up a faint signal from 3-WE, generally soaked in static and overlapped with Glenn Miller or Lionel Richie tunes coming from God knows where. On countless winter nights, with a biting wind scraping barren branches against the paint-chipped windows of a family room that genuinely felt like a meat locker from November through March, I'd lay my head against a speaker and allow the inherent drama of a basketball game play out in the cozy arena of my imagination.

During these years, I became good friends with Joe Tait—whom I never met and, for a time, couldn't pick out of a police lineup. It was the voice of the Cavs' legendary broadcaster that served as a constant, becoming the anchor my ear would latch to as I slowly adjusted the radio dial like a seasoned safecracker. And once I found it, I allowed myself a moment of inner rejoice, knowing I was now about to be treated to an evening of entertainment with a reliable old friend. Whom I didn't know. And couldn't describe.

I suppose this is where my appreciation for the most ordinary of ordinary hatched. While most fans bemoaned (and still bemoan) the preposterous Sahara Desert-length of the NBA season to the point of proclaiming that, for example, a Tuesday night game in January is utterly meaningless, I looked at it completely differently. Any game I could pick up and listen to on the radio— think of it, actually hearing what was happening *as it happened,* not having to wait until the next morning!—was an event that would turn a Tuesday in January into New Year's Eve. And from that foundation, even as cable evolved and the Internet exploded, I still could find appreciation for the apparently meaningless. Now—still out of town—I can watch every single Cavs game on television, follow every basket on a laptop computer, or listen to every single second on a radio broadcast as clear and crisp as a John Denver song about mountains. It's an embarrassment of riches I would have killed for at age fifteen. And, human nature being what it is, I haven't followed the Cavs anywhere near as passionately since it became so ridiculously easy to do so.

Yet I'm glad that mentality has persevered, nurturing the interest to create the book you're about to read. Not every NBA game has playoff implications, and somebody isn't always going to score sixty points (unless it was Michael Jordan playing the Cavs). But each game played is a story. Some incredible, some heartbreaking, and yes indeed, some teeter on utter meaninglessness. But with a healthy appreciation for all, it becomes more satisfying to recognize the truly special—in this case, by ranking the fifty greatest Cavaliers' games of all time.

To be sure, the Cavs do not have a particularly rich history. There are just a few lonely banners of achievement that drift amidst the air ducts high above the floor at (gulp) Quicken Loans Arena. From a greasy downtown tenement to a concrete palace in a pasture to a glistening jewel back downtown, the Cavs franchise has followed a winding road filled with several pretty embarrassing potholes. But in between, there has been some remarkable scenery: the franchise's first tangible baby steps, an incredible renaissance from rock bottom, the arrival of a hometown savior, and a miracle in the meadows that just may represent the greatest moment in Cleveland sports history. Even if the vehicle may not be first-class, fans deserve to enjoy the ride. Love it or hate it, it's our history, and it deserves recognition.

Whether you have courtside seats close enough to breathe in the talcum powder LeBron James tosses into the air before every game or tune in on a rickety old radio picking up a signal from 250 miles away, each Cavs game means something. Accordingly, so do the fifty stories you hold in your hands. I hope the following pages can represent a grammatical photo album of a kooky but lovable family—one for which inclusion is worth laying on an icy floor and pressing your ear to a dusty speaker on a Tuesday night in January.

Golden Victory

In their primarily pathetic first four years of existence, the Cavs had endured more than their share of humiliating, one-sided defeats. Still, there had been gradual improvement, and as the 1974–75 season began, the Cavs appeared on the brink of becoming a bona fide playoff contender, splitting their first fourteen games. While the team had picked up impressive wins here and there, its fledgling fan base—now forced to trek out to Summit County to watch home games—was still waiting for the first exclamation-point victory. When it finally arrived, it came as a surprise not only to the fans but to the Cavs themselves.

The Golden State Warriors arrived at Richfield Coliseum for a Thursday night matchup carrying a 12–5 record—best in the Western Conference—and gripping sole possession of first place in the Pacific Division. Led by versatile forward Rick Barry, who had scored forty-two points in a Warriors' victory at Boston Garden the previous night, Golden State was just getting rolling in what would prove to be the greatest season in franchise history. But on this night, Barry and Company ran into a buzz saw.

The Cavaliers, who had looked listless in losing three of their last four, took charge of the contest from the opening tip, exploding for thirty-one points in the first quarter and surging to a fourteen-point advantage. Guard Bingo Smith, one of the few remaining original Cavs, led the charge with his radar jumper and took Barry out of the game with suffocating defense. Barry, averaging better than thirty-two points per contest, missed all six shots he took in the first twelve minutes. "He was missing some easy shots and that made him mad," Smith said later. "And I tried to play him as tight as I could, stick real close to him."

While Barry struggled, Bingo soared, hitting six of his first eight shots for twelve points in the first quarter. The Warriors hung tough, then Barry broke out of his slump, notching sixteen points in the third quarter to spark the Warriors, who scored the first ten points of the second half to tie the contest.

But unlike so many other times since 1970 when faced with adversity against a superior team, the young Cavaliers did not buckle under pressure. Guard Austin Carr took over, scoring ten points in the next six minutes and tallying fourteen points in the third quarter alone. "I was hesitating, looking for too many things when I got a good shot," said Carr, who would wind up with a game-high twenty-six points. "The guys on the bench noticed it and told me to cut loose." Cut loose he did, helping Cleveland stretch the lead back to seventeen going into the fourth, where the Cavs turned the lights out on the Warriors. Not only did they stymie Golden State's potent offense but the Cavs nearly doubled their lead, scoring thirty fourth-quarter points to win going away, 106–74. Things were so one-sided that afterward, flabbergasted Cavs' coach Bill Fitch started making excuses for Golden State—which would turn out to be the second-highest-scoring team in the NBA in 1974–75.

No excuses were necessary. On this night, the Cavs were clearly the better team. Barry was limited to twenty-three points—nine below his season average—and the seventy-four points were not only the fewest allowed in the Cavaliers' young history but the Warriors' worst offensive tally in twenty years.

With one unforgettable victory, the Cavs had vaulted into the role of post-season contender, leaving the ashes of countless blowout defeats behind them. And by season's end, their thirty-two-point washout of Golden State would prove even more telling. For the first time, the Cavs found themselves in the thick of the playoff chase, staving off elimination until the final buzzer of the final game. Meanwhile, the Warriors would go on to capture the Western Conference title, then stun the favored Washington Bullets with a dramatic four-game sweep in the NBA Finals.

That fateful night in Richfield turned out to be the worst loss of their golden season.

	1	2	3	4	
Warriors	17	22	20	15	=74
Cavaliers	31	18	27	30	=106

GOLDEN STATE

Player	FG-FGA	FT-FTA	Reb.	Ass.	Pts.
Beard	2–3	0–1	3	2	4
C. Johnson	4–13	3–4	2	2	11
Ray	2–8	3–7	11	0	7
Barry	8–23	7–8	3	4	23
Wilkes	4–14	0–0	15	2	8
Mullins	2–7	0–0	1	2	4
Dickey	0–4	0–0	2	2	0
Dudley	1–3	0–0	2	1	2
G. Johnson	2–3	0–0	5	1	4
Smith	2–7	2–2	0	0	6
Bracey	0–0	0–0	0	0	0
Kendrick	2–3	1–2	2	0	5
TOTAL	29–88	16–24	47	16	74

CLEVELAND

Player	FG-FGA	FT-FTA	Reb.	Ass.	Pts.
Carr	12–20	2–3	1	1	26
Cleamons	0–1	0–0	8	10	0
Chones	5–9	5–8	9	6	15
Smith	11–17	1–2	4	2	23
Davis	3–6	3–4	9	8	9
Snyder	2–6	0–0	1	5	4
Brewer	3–5	6–7	8	2	12
Patterson	1–5	1–2	5	2	3
Foster	4–8	0–0	0	0	8
Walker	1–3	0–0	0	1	2
Witte	0–2	0–0	1	0	0
Russell	2–3	0–0	1	0	4
TOTAL	44–85	18–26	47	37	106

Attendance: 5,811

CAVALIERS 113, BOSTON CELTICS 98
NOVEMBER 22, 1980

Fork in the Road

They were two franchises headed in wildly different directions. One was about to begin arguably the finest stretch of championship-caliber basketball in NBA history and the other was teetering on the brink of becoming the laughingstock of professional sports.

After several lean years to close out the 1970s, the old glory of the Boston Celtics had been reborn with the arrival of a wiry sharpshooter from Indiana State University by the name of Larry Bird. In his rookie season of 1979–80, Bird sparked Boston to an incredible thirty-two-game turnaround in a sixty-win-season—the first of six the Celtics would notch in the next seven years. With the arrival of soon-to-be-iconic forward Kevin McHale and center Robert Parish for the 1980–81 campaign, the Celtics were on the brink of a dynasty with perhaps the greatest frontcourt in basketball history in place. Though the Celtics were off to a relatively modest 13–5 start, they would rack up sixty-two victories by season's end and Bird and Company would hoist their first banner up into the haunted rafters of Boston Garden. It would not be their last. The Celtics would go on to win four Eastern Conference crowns and two more NBA titles in the next six years as Boston redefined itself as the marquee franchise in basketball.

Meanwhile, the Cavs' unforgettable run to glory in the mid-1970s had flamed out, and by the fall of 1980, not a single player remained from the Miracle of Richfield drama just four years earlier. While the Cavs had struggled, they'd managed to keep their heads above water and at least compete. But with the purchase of the team by bewildered Ted Stepien and his hiring of deluded Bill Musselman as coach, dark days loomed over the horizon for the once-beloved franchise.

The Cavs staggered out of the gate, posting a 6–16 mark over the first six weeks. Thus, when the largest crowd of the season trekked to the Richfield Coliseum for a Saturday night contest with Boston, there was little doubt the bulk of the 8,000-plus was there to see the mighty Celtics rather than the whimpering home team—particularly since Boston had annihilated the Cavs by twenty-seven points on opening night.

Going against all logic, Cleveland roared to a ten-point first-quarter lead, outrunning the Celtics with an aggressive fast break offense. Veteran Cleveland guard Randy Smith, playing in his 700th consecutive game, overcame a sprained left ankle to score twenty-one of his game-high twenty-eight points in the tone-setting first half. Simultaneously, Cavs' forward Kenny Carr led the defensive charge on the other end of the floor. "If you're going to stop Boston," Carr noted, "you have to stop Bird." And stop him he did, limiting Bird to twelve points on the night as he hit just five of sixteen field goals.

While Parish scored twenty-one points, McHale was held to a harmless four and two rebounds as Cleveland coasted to a fourteen-point second-quarter lead. Then, after Boston sliced the deficit to five at the intermission, Carr outscored Bird 12–4 in the critical third period and forward Roger Phegley—one of six Cleveland players to score double figures—exploded for ten points in the fourth as the Cavs pulled away for a win they felt they had to have. "We had to do it tonight," Carr said. "Northeastern Ohio has been on our back, literally. We had to do something and we beat one of the best teams in the East."

"This was real good for the guys, for their confidence," Musselman said afterward. "This was great after what they have gone through."

And, with 218 painful and often embarrassing losses yet to come in the next four seasons, perhaps also for what they were *about* to go through.

	1	2	3	4	
Celtics	26	31	20	21	=98
Cavaliers	36	26	25	26	=113

BOSTON

Player	FG-FGA	FT-FTA	Reb.	Ass.	Pts.
Bird	5–16	2–2	8	4	12
Maxwell	6–10	2–2	4	2	14
Parish	9–13	3–3	7	1	21
Archibald	3–10	4–4	3	8	10
Ford	7–15	2–4	3	5	17
Robey	2–3	0–0	4	1	4
McHale	2–4	0–0	2	1	4
Henderson	5–9	1–2	2	0	11
Fernsten	1–3	3–4	2	1	5
Kreklow	0–2	0–0	1	0	0
TOTAL	40–85	17–21	36	23	98

3-Point Goal: Ford

CLEVELAND

Player	FG-FGA	FT-FTA	Reb.	Ass.	Pts.
Carr	8–14	6–6	10	4	22
Mitchell	10–21	1–2	7	3	21
Laimbeer	4–7	2–2	8	3	10
Bratz	7–12	0–0	1	7	14
Smith	9–17	10–11	3	6	28
Ford	1–3	0–0	1	0	2
Phegley	6–16	0–0	5	1	12
Washington	1–3	0–0	1	1	2
Hughes	0–3	0–0	6	1	0
Lambert	1–1	0–0	0	0	2
Kinch	0–0	0–0	0	0	0
TOTAL	47–97	19–21	42	26	113

Attendance: 8,252

In Your Face

Seemingly overnight, the Cavs had gone from a milquetoast .500 team to the best in basketball. With a young core in place that included center Brad Daugherty, forward John "Hot Rod" Williams, and guards Mark Price and Ron Harper, Cleveland had put together what Magic Johnson predicted would become "the team of the '90s."

After sneaking into the playoffs with a 42–40 record the year before, the Cavs exploded out of the gate in 1988–89. They won twenty of their first twenty-five and rode a ten-game winning streak into a benchmark game against the perennially tough New York Knicks on a cold Saturday night in Richfield.

While the Cavs had flash and flair, it was the gritty underbelly of the team that had sparked this sudden success. As the midpoint of the season neared, Cleveland had the best defensive scoring average in the NBA and, consequently, boasted the largest average margin of victory. And the catalyst behind this surge was a soft-spoken veteran forward who'd been with the team less than a year.

Larry Nance had spent a quiet six seasons with the Phoenix Suns before coming to Cleveland in a midseason trade that sent away promising guard Kevin Johnson and fan-favorite center Mark West. Cleveland fans were perplexed. Few knew Nance had been among the league leaders in blocked shots and field goal percentage since his arrival in the NBA in 1981. His only real claim to fame was winning the first-ever Slam Dunk Contest, but even that was before a tongue-wagging guard from Chicago redefined the art. Yet Nance was an integral part of the 1987–88 Cavs' late-season charge that notched a playoff berth. Now, with the athletic and graceful Nance clogging up the lane, the

Cavs' defense had become fierce and unforgiving. And Nance's impact—both on opponents and his own teammates—was never more apparent than on this night against the first-place Knicks.

Still smarting from a fifteen-point defeat to New York two months earlier, the Cavs came into the contest with something to prove. Five seconds into the game, Nance swatted away a shot attempt by seven-foot New York center Patrick Ewing, and the tone had been set for a historic evening before 20,000 witnesses at the Coliseum.

The Knicks inexplicably continued to challenge Nance, and time and again he would turn their shots away. "They just kept coming at me and I just kept blocking them," he said. And even when he didn't get a hand on the ball, he still made good things happen. "Even if he doesn't block their shots," Cleveland guard Craig Ehlo noted, "he makes them think the next time they come down the lane."

Altogether, Nance made the Knicks think eleven times on the night—a team record—and tallied just over half of the team's twenty-one blocked shots for the game, which tied the NBA mark. In one two-minute stretch, the Knicks put up four shots from close range—and all four were blocked. But the biggest swat of the night came in the waning minutes. After New York had cut a seventeen-point deficit to six, Nance deflected a short jumper by Sidney Green, then stuffed a putback attempt by Gerald Wilkins. The second block led to a fast break and a Ron Harper slam dunk that put the game away. For good measure, on New York's next possession, Nance blocked a layup attempt by guard Mark Jackson. The crowd loved every second of it. "Larry Nance was a defensive monster in the lane today," Cavs' coach Lenny Wilkens said.

When Nance came out of the game with sixteen seconds left, he received a thunderous standing ovation. In addition to his menagerie of blocks, he scored twenty-four points, snagged six rebounds, and dished out four assists as the Cavs improved their record to an uncanny 24–5 on the strength of their eleventh straight victory, a franchise record.

These Cavs were providing their fans with a brand of basketball they'd never seen before. And no one played a more significant role than the lean giant down low with his socks pulled up to his knees and his hand in every opponent's face.

	1	2	3	4	
Knicks	26	29	18	23	=96
Cavaliers	31	26	26	21	=104

NEW YORK

Player	FG-FGA	FT-FTA	Reb.	Ass.	Pts.
Newman	2–9	2–2	2	1	6
Oakley	6–14	2–3	11	4	14
Ewing	9–16	3–3	5	1	21
G. Wilkins	1–14	1–2	3	1	3
Jackson	6–17	1–3	5	8	13
Tucker	8–8	0–0	4	1	17
Strickland	4–5	0–0	2	1	8
Walker	1–6	0–0	1	0	2
Green	4–8	1–1	8	0	9
E. Wilkins	1–3	1–2	2	0	3
TOTAL	42–100	11–16	43	17	96

3-Point Goals: 1–10 (Tucker 1–1, G. Wilkins 0–4, Newman 0–3, Jackson 0–1, Walker 0–1)

CLEVELAND

Player	FG-FGA	FT-FTA	Reb.	Ass.	Pts.
Sanders	5–11	0–0	5	1	10
Nance	10–15	4–4	6	4	24
Daugherty	4–11	4–9	12	5	12
Harper	10–19	8–10	11	7	30
Price	5–11	1–3	9	7	11
Williams	4–7	3–4	3	0	11
Ehlo	1–3	0–0	4	3	2
Valentine	1–1	0–0	0	0	2
Dudley	0–1	2–4	0	0	2
TOTAL	40–79	22–34	50	27	104

3-Point Goals: 2–5 (Harper 2–5)

Attendance: 20,013

#47

CAVALIERS 113, PORTLAND TRAIL BLAZERS 101
MARCH 4, 1977

All Grown Up

They were born into the NBA like twin brothers—two fledging expansion franchises with big dreams and little talent, planted in geographic areas starved for a winner. They played one another early and often in their historic first campaigns and suffered side by side through a string of long, learning seasons. In their first five years, the Cavaliers and Portland Trail Blazers combined to lose more than 500 games as they both desperately struggled to shed the "expansion" label.

But in the 1975–76 season, the Cavs turned a corner, posting their first winning record and notching their initial playoff berth. And while Cleveland was fighting its way back to the postseason the following year, the Blazers had embarked on what still stands as the greatest season in franchise history. As the teams prepared to square off for the thirty-eighth time in their young histories, the once-hopeless newcomers had both established themselves not only as legitimate playoff contenders but as two of the most respected franchises in the game.

Battling the Los Angeles Lakers for first in the Pacific Division, Portland had finally put it all together. Former UCLA center Bill Walton had come of age and veteran forward Maurice Lucas packed the scoring punch the Trail Blazers had lacked. Meanwhile, the Cavs continued to compete despite a handful of key injuries, showcasing valuable depth that had eluded them for years and jousting with Washington for a second straight Central Division title.

An otherwise ordinary regular-season contest bore special meaning for both teams and their fans, as better than 12,000 packed into Portland's Memorial Coliseum to watch these now-mature squads do battle. Though Walton was out with a sprained ankle, Portland's depth cushioned his absence, as seven players scored in double figures. But this night belonged to the Cavs, who had struggled mightily on the road all season—evidenced by their blowing a twenty-four-point lead in a loss at Philadelphia two weeks before.

The contest was tight early, with ten lead changes and nine ties in the first half. But after the Blazers snuck to a 40–39 lead in the second quarter, Cleveland exploded for the next ten points and never again trailed. The margin swelled to fourteen in the third, then nineteen in the fourth as the Cavs' own depth took center stage. Seven of their players hit double digits as well, led by red-hot forward Campy Russell, who scored a game-high twenty-six points. Meanwhile, fellow forward Jim Brewer dominated Lucas, holding him to fifteen points and only six field goals in twenty-two attempts. The Cavaliers also got an unexpected lift off the bench from a pair of unlikely players. Guard Gary Brokaw doubled his season average with fourteen points while dishing out five assists, while recently acquired center Elmore Smith ripped down thirteen rebounds and blocked four shots alongside eleven points. Neither played more than twenty minutes.

Appropriately, Cleveland's victory knotted the all-time series between the expansion siblings at nineteen wins apiece. Yet it also marked the beginning of one of the greatest chapters in the history of the City of Roses—Blazermania. Portland would not lose another game at Memorial Coliseum for the remainder of the season, ripping off wins in its final seven home dates, then, playing before raucous crowds in the playoffs, the Blazers were a perfect ten-for-ten on their home court as they notched upsets over Denver, Los Angeles, and Philadelphia to become the youngest team ever to win an NBA crown. The home winning streak would stretch to an incredible forty-three games the following season, but perhaps more telling, shortly after the Cavs' victory in March, a sellout streak at Memorial Coliseum began, not to end for two decades.

Just as the Miracle of Richfield had announced the Cavaliers' arrival among the league elite, the Blazers' unforgettable run to the '77 title—begun immediately after the Cavs' final visit to Portland that season—did the same for the Trail Blazers. The two infant franchises, once mercilessly teased and embarrassingly tattered, were all grown up.

	1	2	3	4	
Cavaliers	21	34	30	28	=113
Trail Blazers	21	27	29	24	=101

CLEVELAND

Player	FG-FGA	FT-FTA	Reb.	Ass.	Pts.
Russell	9–16	8–9	6	5	26
Brewer	3–7	0–0	7	3	6
Chones	3–12	0–0	8	2	6
Walker	5–6	0–2	2	4	10
Carr	5–6	1–1	2	2	11
Snyder	6–15	4–5	3	3	16
B. Smith	6–11	1–1	4	4	13
Brokaw	6–10	2–2	1	5	14
E. Smith	5–7	1–3	13	1	11
Williams	0–0	0–0	0	0	0
TOTAL	48–90	17–23	46	29	113

PORTLAND

Player	FG-FGA	FT-FTA	Reb.	Ass.	Pts.
Lucas	6–22	3–5	12	6	15
Gross	6–8	5–6	6	4	17
Jones	5–13	4–5	7	1	14
Hollins	2–9	0–1	2	2	4
Twardzik	5–9	4–4	6	0	14
Steele	4–10	3–3	1	1	11
Gilliam	6–13	1–1	3	5	13
Neal	5–8	0–0	8	1	10
Davis	0–1	0–0	2	3	0
Walker	0–1	3–5	0	0	3
Calhoun	0–0	0–0	0	0	0
TOTAL	39–94	23–30	47	23	101

Attendance: 12,202

CAVALIERS 110, GOLDEN STATE WARRIORS 106
JANUARY 27, 1982

One-Night Stand

In the middle of the darkest chapter in franchise history, beams of sunlight—or even silver-lined clouds—were hard to come by.

In the midst of Ted Stepien's disastrous reign as team owner, the Cavs had plummeted to the worst team in basketball during the 1981–82 season, losing thirty-three of their first forty games. By season's end, four different men would serve as head coach and twenty-three different players would take the floor as Cleveland matched its worst record in franchise history, closing the campaign with an incredible nineteen-game losing streak.

But on an unforgettable January night, one player made all that misery disappear with one of the most incredible individual achievements in NBA history.

The Golden State Warriors were some fifteen games better than Cleveland when the teams tipped off before a miniscule crowd at Richfield Coliseum in an utterly meaningless contest. And, led by flamboyant scoring machine World B. Free, the Warriors surged to a ten-point lead in the first quarter. The script for yet another Cavaliers loss was being followed to the letter.

But rather than folding, the Cavs showed unusual resiliency and rallied to tie the contest at the half, then surged ahead in the third quarter. The catalyst was Geoff Huston, a young guard Stepien acquired in one of his countless buffoonish trades. Though just six-foot-two, Huston played like a giant, taking over every aspect of the game. The team-high twenty-four points he scored were impressive, but not nearly as notable as what he accomplished as a passer. Huston, dishing to open teammates time and again, racked up a team-record twenty-seven assists—shattering the old Cleveland record of twenty and falling just two shy of the league mark. Huston alone notched seven more assists than the entire Golden State team. "Geoff really played well," said Chuck Daly, the third of the Cavs' quartet of coaches that season. "He started going to the basket and they backed off of him, then he burned them."

As if his offensive heroics weren't enough, Huston also smothered Free on the other end of the court. After scoring fourteen points in the first quarter, Free—who had been a high school teammate of Huston in Brooklyn—was held to eight the rest of the night as the Cavaliers gained the upper hand.

Appropriately, a Huston pass to center Bill Laimbeer for a layup ignited Cleveland's final run down the stretch. Forward James Edwards hit a critical fall-away six-footer with a minute left to put the Cavs up by one, then forward Scott Wedman—playing his first game after missing a month with a broken foot—hit a twenty-foot shot to clinch a four-point win. It was Cleveland's first home triumph in five weeks. "The only way you can stop the controversy is win," Huston said afterward, "so it was time for a win tonight. All you can do is come out and play, and that's what I did."

Huston never again matched the shining potential he displayed that night. And the Cavs' return to normalcy wouldn't truly begin for another three years, long after Stepien had departed and his senseless personnel decisions finally began to fade like an infected rash.

But for one memorable evening, the forlorn Cleveland Cavaliers were a competitive team with a promising young star.

	1	2	3	4	
Warriors	36	26	24	20	=106
Cavaliers	26	36	25	23	=110

GOLDEN STATE

Player	FG-FGA	FT-FTA	Reb.	Ass.	Pts.
King	12–22	5–7	5	2	29
Smith	2–2	0–0	6	1	4
Carroll	3–8	1–3	8	0	7
Gale	1–7	1–1	2	3	3
Free	9–21	4–5	2	7	22
Parker	1–1	2–2	3	1	4
Brown	1–3	2–2	8	0	4
Romar	1–2	0–0	0	2	2
Short	10–17	3–4	9	4	24
Hassett	2–6	0–0	1	0	5
Lloyd	1–1	0–0	0	0	2
TOTAL	43–90	18–24	44	20	106

3-Point Goals: Short, Hassett

CLEVELAND

Player	FG-FGA	FT-FTA	Reb.	Ass.	Pts.
Johnson	3–4	4–6	3	0	10
Carr	7–12	5–8	13	1	19
Edwards	10–21	2–2	7	3	22
Huston	10–17	4–6	1	27	24
Brewer	7–17	3–5	5	1	17
Laimbeer	2–3	0–0	3	1	4
Wedman	4–6	0–2	3	1	8
Herron	3–4	0–0	0	0	6
Wilkerson	0–1	0–0	1	0	0
TOTAL	46–85	18–29	36	34	110

Attendance: 4,184

CAVALIERS 117, NEW YORK KNICKS 112 (OT)
OCTOBER 25, 1977

Cool Clyde

Perhaps never before in the history of professional sports had there been a more literal or dramatic example of the city mouse being relocated to the country.

In his ten years with the New York Knicks, guard Walt "Clyde" Frazier had become the living embodiment of "cool." From his big hats and fur coats to his swank apartment with mirrors on the ceiling to his decked-out Rolls Royce, Frazier was the quintessential 1970s pro athlete—a silky-smooth master of the urban landscape who helped lead the Knicks to eight playoff appearances and a pair of NBA titles.

Thus, when the seven-time All-Star found himself calling sleepy Richfield, Ohio, home in the fall of 1977, he'd come face-to-face with culture shock. After losing guard Jim Cleamons to New York as a free agent, the Cavaliers received the thirty-two-year-old Frazier as ironic compensation. While Frazier's lifestyle may have taken an unwelcome 180-degree turn, his production remained steadfast in the first week of the 1977–78 season as he gave the Cavs everything they could have hoped for: averaging seventeen points, five rebounds, and five assists in the first three games. Thus, Frazier—if not the 1–2 Cavaliers—brought momentum into his old stomping ground of Madison Square Garden, where he was often booed in his final two seasons with the Knicks. What followed that October night was what *Plain Dealer* reporter Bill Nichols described as "a homecoming usually seen in a Hollywood epic."

Before a capacity crowd of 19,694 under the hallowed rafters—the earliest Knicks' sellout in four years—Frazier put on a show few thought he was still capable of. Led by his swashbuckling on-court confidence, the Cavs matched the Knicks blow-for-blow in a contest that was tied twenty-one times and saw fourteen lead changes. Though they'd lost sixteen of the seventeen games they'd played at Madison Square Garden, the Cavs vaulted to a six-point lead in the fourth quarter, then clawed back to a 105–103 advantage when Bingo Smith drilled a pair of free throws with nine seconds remaining. But New York center Bob McAdoo answered with a pair of foul shots with three ticks showing to send the game to overtime, where the Knicks seemed certain to pull out victory.

Instead, Smith hit three long jumpers to open the extra frame, then Frazier came up with a big steal and a three-point play to give Cleveland enough momentum to secure a 117–112 triumph. As the final seconds ticked down, a beaming Frazier dribbled the ball at midcourt with his left hand while pumping his right fist triumphantly in the air. The antagonistic New York crowd rose to its feet to give its former hero a well-deserved standing ovation. Frazier was smoother than ever on this night, exploding for twenty-eight points, eight rebounds, five steals, and four assists in one of the greatest performances in his illustrious career. "I'm just glad I can come back and play a game like this," Frazier said. "This game gave me the same satisfaction I had when we won two titles."

"The script was made for Walt," Cavs' coach Bill Fitch said afterward. "It was a beautiful game with a happy ending." Fitch's words were true in more ways than one. As it happened, Frazier's return to New York also marked the last chapter of glory in his memorable career. He would miss thirty games to injury that season, then appear in just fifteen more over the next two seasons. Players grumbled he was a prima donna, while the front office inferred Frazier was faking a foot injury simply because he didn't like playing in Cleveland. Meanwhile, the media attacked him for not sitting on the bench during the games he'd miss, though in reality he was in the locker room receiving treatment on his injured foot. The Cavs finally released him in 1979 and few basketball aficionados even recall Frazier's stint in wine and gold.

Yet for one magical night in the Big Apple, the Cavs had a Hall of Fame player in their corner.

	1	2	3	4	OT	
Cavaliers	21	28	32	24	12	=117
Knicks	21	28	26	30	7	=112

CLEVELAND

Player	FG-FGA	FT-FTA	Reb.	Ass.	Pts.
Brewer	0–3	2–4	4	2	2
Russell	7–15	14–17	8	8	28
Chones	7–12	2–3	6	3	16
Frazier	12–21	4–4	8	4	28
Walker	2–8	0–2	3	0	4
Carr	6–13	3–3	5	2	15
E. Smith	3–7	1–4	7	1	7
B. Smith	6–12	3–3	4	1	15
Jordan	0–1	0–0	1	1	0
Lambert	1–2	0–0	4	0	2
TOTAL	44–94	29–40	50	22	117

NEW YORK

Player	FG-FGA	FT-FTA	Reb.	Ass.	Pts.
Haywood	6–12	2–3	13	3	14
McMillan	2–4	3–4	4	4	7
McAdoo	9–25	11–16	11	2	29
Beard	5–8	2–2	3	3	12
Monroe	5–15	4–4	2	3	14
Williams	3–4	4–7	0	4	10
Knight	5–7	1–1	3	1	11
Shelton	3–4	3–6	10	3	9
Cleamons	2–5	0–0	3	2	4
Gondrezick	0–1	0–0	1	2	0
Jackson	1–1	0–0	0	1	2
TOTAL	41–86	30–43	50	28	112

Attendance: 19,694

CAVALIERS 100, ORLANDO MAGIC 99 (OT)
FEBRUARY 15, 1995

Fratello's Fingerprints

In a flash, the Cavs were on the brink of putting an exclamation point on a remarkable victory.

Coming off a miserable loss in Boston in which they'd only managed to score sixty-seven points, the Cavaliers defied expectation and had controlled the NBA's finest team from the opening tip before a rocking sellout crowd at brand-new Gund Arena. Seemingly overnight, the Orlando Magic had developed into a title contender, thanks to the arrival of youngsters Shaquille O'Neal and Anfernee Hardaway and veteran forward Horace Grant. The resurgent Magic had cruised to a 38–10 start in 1994–95 and would wind up representing the Eastern Conference in the NBA Finals. Orlando had dominated the Cavaliers in back-to-back meetings in December, but on a cold February night in downtown Cleveland, the Magic appeared to be no match for the fiery Cavs.

Gritty performances like these were nothing new to the Cavaliers in their second year under coach Mike Fratello. They'd persevered through countless injuries and setbacks the year before and still managed to reach the playoffs, thanks to their quick, aggressive play. What Fratello's Cavs lacked in consistency, they made up for with hustle and hard work. It was a team that matched the personality of its flamboyant and intense head coach, who had already made an indelible mark on what had in recent years become a successful but phlegmatic franchise.

Fratello's fingerprints were all over this matchup with the Magic. Cleveland took control early, carrying a seven-point lead into the second half. But Orlando showed the reserve that would take it to the Finals, rallying to tie the contest when forward Dennis Scott drilled a three-point shot with 12.3

25

seconds remaining. On the Cavs' final possession, battered forward Tyrone Hill—playing with both hands heavily taped—slipped behind the Orlando defense and leapt up to slam home the winning basket. But Hill's thunderous conclusion to a well-played game went awry when the ball slipped out of his hand and bounded off the back of the rim. The Cavs' certain victory had vanished and they would now have to battle the Magic in overtime—Cleveland's sixth extra session of the season. "It was at a point," Fratello admitted later, "where it could easily slip away."

Sure enough, Orlando quickly jumped to a four-point advantage on back-to-back baskets by O'Neal and Scott. But, as they'd already done a handful of times in Fratello's short tenure, the Cavs dug deep and refused to surrender. Terrell Brandon, playing one of the finest games of his career, took control. First he halted the Magic momentum with a three-point play to cut the margin to one. Just over a minute later he tied the game at ninety-eight with a driving layup, then scored what turned out to be the game-winning points with a pair of free throws with 21.8 seconds left. The small but dashing point guard from Oregon scored a career-high thirty-one points, hitting twelve of fifteen field goals while dishing out eight assists.

Orlando had one final chance to win, but Hardaway's fallaway fifteen-footer over Bobby Phills fell short at the buzzer, and the Cavs had picked up the biggest win in the brief history of their new arena. "It was a tremendous performance," Fratello said. "I can't tell you how happy I am for the team. I'm really excited that they came back to hold on to get that win."

It was also more than a typical night for Fratello, who picked up his 400th career victory. Afterward he had each Cavs player and coach sign a game ball to commemorate a game to remember—both for the coach and the franchise.

	1	2	3	4	OT	
Magic	16	27	21	27	8	=99
Cavaliers	22	28	20	21	9	=100

ORLANDO

Player	FG-FGA	FT-FTA	Reb.	Ass.	Pts.
Royal	3–4	3–6	2	0	9
Grant	7–12	1–2	8	1	15
O'Neal	9–17	8–14	9	3	26
Hardaway	4–13	0–1	3	9	9
Anderson	4–10	1–2	9	3	10
Scott	6–13	3–4	5	5	19
Rollins	0–0	0–0	0	0	0
Shaw	0–3	0–0	4	1	0
Avent	3–3	0–0	0	0	6
Bowie	2–2	0–0	0	2	5
TOTAL	38–77	16–29	40	24	99

3-Point Goals: 7–19 (Scott 4–8, Bowie 1–1, Anderson 1–2, Hardaway 1–6, O'Neal 0–1, Shaw 0–1)

CLEVELAND

Player	FG-FGA	FT-FTA	Reb.	Ass.	Pts.
Mills	5–15	0–0	6	3	12
Hill	5–16	2–6	17	2	12
Williams	3–12	4–4	5	4	10
Brandon	12–15	5–5	4	8	31
Phills	3–8	0–2	1	2	7
Cage	1–3	0–0	4	0	2
Dreiling	1–2	0–0	1	0	2
Ferry	6–7	0–0	1	1	15
Colter	0–1	2–2	0	3	2
Campbell	2–3	2–2	0	0	7
TOTAL	38–82	15–21	39	23	100

3-Point Goals: 9–13 (Ferry 3–4, Brandon 2–2, Mills 2–4, Phills 1–1, Campbell 1–1, Colter 0–1)

Attendance: 20,562

CAVALIERS 114, PHILADELPHIA 76ERS 101
DECEMBER 27, 1970

The Lovable Losers Strike Back

By the midpoint of the Cavaliers' inaugural season, the team had already experienced enough humiliation to last the remainder of the decade. They'd won just four of their first forty-one games, and each of those meager victories was against fellow expansion squads Buffalo and Portland—both of which were off to significantly better starts.

Cleveland was so bad that the team became something of an underprivileged mascot. When public-address announcers would read scores at arenas around the league, fans would attentively listen for the Cavs' score. If they were winning—or even tied—the crowd would begin to cheer. It was some of the only cheering the luckless team was getting at the time, since the Cavs were drawing an average of just 2,500 per home game at musty Cleveland Arena, including a modest 6,144 for the historic inaugural contest. The hope that fans would flock to see the new team had already evaporated. "Cleveland's fans have been drenched with failure for too long to react that way," Bob Dolgan wrote in the *Plain Dealer*. "That's why they'll only support winners." And keep in mind, this was only 1970. There was a lot more failure on the horizon for Cleveland to be drenched with.

Many fans were also growing weary of the Cavs' ridiculously poor play. It was a very different scenario from the icon of hopeless expansion teams, Major League Baseball's 1962 New York Mets, who were so hapless they became both entertaining and beloved. The Cavaliers actually had some talent and a few promising players—they just played bad basketball. And their brand of basketball had never been worse than in their eleventh game, when Cleveland was absolutely annihilated in Philadelphia, 141–87—a fifty-four-point pounding that epitomized the misery of the entire season. So embarrassed by the performance, Bill Fitch fined each player $54 afterward—one dollar for each point the team lost by.

Two days after Christmas, the teams met again, this time in Cleveland. Appropriately, just over 2,200 fans filed through the turnstiles for what everyone figured would be another bloodletting. Though the Sixers had plane trouble in Philadelphia and didn't arrive in Cleveland until 7:20 for a scheduled 8 P.M. tip, it was the Cavs who looked sluggish. After an hour delay, the Sixers sprinted to an early 16–6 lead and took a ten-point advantage into the second quarter. But instead of succumbing to yet another defeat, the Cavaliers fought back with a thirty-point second period and took the lead just before the half. With rookies Joe Cooke, Bingo Smith, John Warren, and Luther Rackley leading the turnaround off the bench, the miniscule crowd began to get into the game. But they soon settled down again when the home team came out lethargic in the second half, scoring just four points in the first six minutes of the third quarter. Again, it looked as if Philadelphia would coast. But once more, the upstart Cavaliers refused to quit. They exploded for twenty points in the final six minutes of the period and took a one-point lead into the fourth. And now, the gathering of just over 2,000 sounded five times as big.

In the final stanza, the Cavs looked like anything but an expansion team. Cooke hit five of six shots and scored all of his thirteen points in the final twelve minutes, joining Smith's sixteen and Warren's ten second-half points. As a team, Cleveland shot a remarkable sixteen of twenty-two in the fourth period—a clip of 73 percent—as the squad showed a balance unseen over the first half of the season, scoring a whopping thirty-nine points in the final twelve minutes. The Cavs went ahead for good on a tip-in by forward Dave Sorenson with 10:23 remaining and never looked back, roaring to a thirteen-point victory—a sixty-seven-point turnaround from their first meeting eight weeks before. For the first time, beat writer Bill Nichols wrote, the Cavs had "socked it to the establishment."

"This let us know we can beat the good teams," Smith said, words that took on added meaning when the Sixers went on to win forty-seven games and qualify for the playoffs. It was the Cavs' first win over a nonexpansion team and, combined with a win over Buffalo the night before, also marked their first back-to-back triumphs.

"I reminded them of the first game," Fitch admitted afterward. "Yes, I pumped them up a little tonight. I'd say they had an incentive." And appropriately, the coach refunded each player's $54 fine.

	1	2	3	4	
76ers	32	22	20	27	=101
Cavaliers	22	30	24	38	=114

PHILADELPHIA

Player	FG	FT-FTA	Pts.
Washington	5	6–7	16
Greer	6	0–1	12
Awtrey	2	4–4	8
Clark	12	1–2	25
Cunningham	10	5–7	25
Jackson	0	2–2	2
Howell	1	2–2	4
Dierkling	1	0–0	2
Foster	2	3–4	7
TOTAL	39	23–29	101

CLEVELAND

Player	FG	FT-FTA	Pts.
Lewis	2	2–3	6
Johnson	7	3–3	17
Wesley	5	0–0	10
Sorenson	7	7–8	21
McLemore	3	0–0	6
Smith	7	4–4	18
Cooke	5	3–5	13
Rackley	4	3–5	11
Warren	6	0–0	12
TOTAL	46	22–28	114

Attendance: 2,282

CHICAGO BULLS 95, CAVALIERS 92 (OT)
MAY 3, 1994

A Better Fate

In the twenty years they'd resided in the Richfield Coliseum, the Cavaliers had experienced some incredible highs and more than their share of unspeakable lows. It was where the team had grown up, learned to become a winner, then lost everything, and again rebuilt into a title contender. With the beginning of the 1994–95 campaign, the team would tip off at brand-new Gund Arena in downtown Cleveland and the Coliseum would sit primarily silent in a Richfield meadow until it was finally destroyed in 1999. It seemed only appropriate that the team's final game in the "Big Arena on the Prairie" served as a microcosm of the ups and downs of the previous two decades.

Mike Fratello's first season as coach in 1993–94 had been flooded by adversity. All season, the Cavaliers were beset by an almost biblical plague of injuries as only one player appeared in more than eighty games. Still, the Cavs fought through it, rallying for thirty-four victories in their final fifty-one games to qualify for the playoffs for the third straight year. And for the third straight year, they would face the mighty Chicago Bulls. But these Bulls were a completely different franchise from the one that had captured the previous three NBA titles. With star guard Michael Jordan's sudden retirement and bizarre foray into minor-league baseball, Chicago's supporting cast was forced to step to the forefront. And it did, posting an impressive 55–27 record. Still, many Cleveland writers and fans figured the Cavs matched up well with the Bulls, evidenced by three victories in four games with Chicago during the regular season.

Hopes for an upset went up in smoke just before the best-of-five series began when forward John "Hot Rod" Williams was sidelined with a broken thumb. He joined battered center Brad Daugherty and forward Larry Nance on the sideline—making an unavailable trio that had combined to average better than forty points per game in the regular season. Making matters worse, Cleveland guard Bobby Phills would only see limited playing time with a scratched cornea.

Not surprisingly, the Bulls coasted to comfortable victories in the first two games in Chicago and the teams traveled to Richfield for Game Three on a cool spring night with the Bulls looking to put the series away and the Cavs simply hoping to live to fight another day. And as they'd done all season, the Cavaliers hung tough. They took a four-point lead to the half and then built the margin to eight late in the third period. But Chicago ripped off a 16–0 run to take its own eight-point advantage early in the fourth, and the weary Cavaliers appeared to be on the ropes.

Yet Fratello's boys had one last charge left in them. Cleveland rallied to tie the game in the final minute and then had a chance to take the last shot with seven-tenths of a second left. On the in-bounds play, Cavs' guard Gerald Wilkins caught the pass and was knocked down by the Bulls' Pete Myers, but official Jess Kersey made no call on the play. Time expired and the teams went to overtime. The non-call was so bad that Chicago forward Scottie Pippen thanked Kersey during the ensuing television time-out.

In the extra session, the plucky Cavaliers finally ran out of gas. A Pippen layup with 1:21 remaining broke a 92–92 tie and gave Chicago a lead it wouldn't relinquish. Still, Cleveland kept fighting and had a chance to extend the game again, but Wilkins missed a three-point shot as time expired.

Perhaps it was only appropriate the Coliseum era ended with a loss to Chicago. The Bulls had, after all, defined the era almost as much as the Cavaliers. The teams had played eleven epic playoff games at Richfield in the building's final six seasons, and the Bulls had won seven—more postseason victories than any other opposing team in Coliseum history. But their average margin of victory, reflected in the final game, was just over four points.

"The guys laid everything they had on the court," said Cleveland guard Mark Price, who overcame a miserable shooting slump in the first two games to score twenty-two points in the Coliseum finale. "My team deserved a better fate," Fratello offered succinctly. "And so, the door closes on a building and an era." As the final buzzer echoed through the hushed Coliseum, it marked not just the end of the season but an unforgettable chapter in Cavalier history.

	1	2	3	4	OT	
Bulls	25	19	27	16	8	=95
Cavaliers	28	20	27	12	5	=92

CHICAGO

Player	FG-FGA	FT-FTA	Reb.	Ass.	Pts.
Pippen	10–22	3–4	11	6	23
Grant	5–12	4–8	6	3	14
Longley	4–8	4–4	6	0	12
Myers	1–4	2–4	1	4	4
Armstrong	5–8	4–5	5	2	14
English	0–1	0–0	0	0	0
Kukoc	6–11	5–6	6	1	18
Williams	2–9	2–2	7	0	6
Kerr	1–2	1–1	1	1	4
Wennington	0–0	0–0	0	0	0
Paxson	0–0	0–0	0	0	0
TOTAL	34–77	25–34	43	17	95

3-Point Goals: 2–8 (Kukoc 1–1, Kerr 1–1, Myers 0–1, English 0–1, Pippen 0–4)

CLEVELAND

Player	FG-FGA	FT-FTA	Reb.	Ass.	Pts.
Mills	10–17	2–2	10	3	25
Hill	5–12	5–13	13	1	15
Kempton	2–9	0–0	9	4	4
Wilkins	3–14	3–4	8	7	10
Price	8–18	5–5	2	5	22
Higgins	1–2	0–0	0	1	3
Brandon	4–5	0–1	2	3	8
Phills	2–8	0–0	5	2	5
TOTAL	35–85	15–25	49	26	92

3-Point Goals: 7–16 (Mills 3–4, Phills 1–1, Higgins 1–2, Price 1–3, Wilkins 1–6)

Attendance: 17,778

CAVALIERS 104, NEW ORLEANS HORNETS 100
FEBRUARY 23, 2004

Down But Not Out

From the opening tip, it was clear it was just going to be one of those nights for the Cavaliers.

The visiting New Orleans Hornets, a perennial playoff squad, came out of the locker room with both barrels blazing, hitting an amazing 78 percent of their shots in the first period as they roared to a twenty-one-point lead on the overwhelmed Cavaliers. Losing to a more talented team was nothing new, but losing in this particular fashion was.

The 22–34 Cavs hadn't whipped up much excitement during the 2003–04 season, aside from the expected interest surrounding rookie LeBron James, but they'd at least managed to stay competitive—a vital quality considering the team had lost at least fifty games in each of the previous four seasons. So getting blown off their home floor in the first quarter was both surprising and uncharacteristic and could have snowballed into utter disaster for a young team on the brink of putting it all together.

And the Hornets didn't let up. When the lead swelled to twenty-five at 49–24 in the second quarter, the Cavs were at the crossroads. They could accept another lopsided defeat or they could try to patiently battle back, possession by possession, shot by shot. An inexperienced team with a first-year coach opted for the latter, and ever so slowly, Cleveland crept back into the game.

The Cavs cut the margin to fourteen at the half, then landed a haymaker in the form of a 20–8 run that made it 67–65, and New Orleans took a meager four-point lead into the final quarter. The home crowd of 17,000-plus, subdued for much of the evening, was finally roaring. And things only got better. Early in the fourth, little-used Cleveland forward Jason Kapono hit back-to-back three-pointers to tie the game. Kapono, who hadn't even played in Cleveland's previous game, hit five three-point shots on the night and scored a season-high nineteen points. Though he would finish the season averaging just over three points in ten minutes per game, Kapono wound up playing twenty-eight minutes on this night, more action than he'd seen in the previous month's games combined.

When guard Jeff McInnis scored to give Cleveland its first lead at 83–82, the crowd nearly exploded. But the Hornets wouldn't quit, and the Cavs would need clutch play down the stretch to ensure their stirring comeback wasn't all for nothing. A three-pointer by McInnis snapped a tie. Then layups by Carlos Boozer and James put Cleveland up by four with less than two minutes to play. Boozer sealed victory in the final twenty-six seconds with a dunk and a pair of free throws, and when the final buzzer sounded, the Cavaliers had notched the most impressive comeback in franchise history. "We never thought at one moment that we were out of the game," said center Tony Battie. "That was the biggest part in pulling out the victory."

The season before, when the Cavs lost sixty-five games, such a comeback would have been unthinkable. And while phenom James played a key role in the turnaround (twenty-one points, six assists) it was anything but a one-man show. Boozer led the team with twenty-four points on just eleven shot attempts and tore down five key offensive rebounds. McInnis dished out a game-high nine assists, and Cleveland only committed nine turnovers for the game while racking up ten blocked shots and thirteen steals. Literally overnight, the Cavaliers had become an entirely different team. "We're finding ways to win," James said afterward. "Even when we were struggling, I said that we were going to come together someway or somehow."

The Hornet comeback began the Cavs' first playoff charge in six years, and though they fell short, the 2003–04 season—and that victory in particular—set the tone for what lay ahead in the years to come.

	1	2	3	4	
Hornets	37	22	18	23	=100
Cavaliers	16	29	28	31	=104

NEW ORLEANS

Player	FG-FGA	FT-FTA	Reb.	Ass.	Pts.
Augmon	3–4	4–4	2	1	10
Brown	6–7	1–2	13	2	13
Magloire	2–10	3–4	7	1	7
Davis	11–21	6–8	5	5	34
Mashburn	9–24	3–4	8	1	23
Armstrong	2–7	0–0	3	3	5
Traylor	1–2	0–0	2	0	2
Lynch	0–0	0–0	2	0	0
West	2–3	2–2	4	3	6
Smith	0–0	0–0	0	0	0
TOTAL	36–78	19–24	46	16	100

3-Point Goals: 9–22 (Davis 6–12, Mashburn 2–5, Armstrong 1–5)

CLEVELAND

Player	FG-FGA	FT-FTA	Reb.	Ass.	Pts.
Newbie	0–1	0–0	0	1	0
Boozer	7–11	10–15	9	1	24
Ilgauskas	7–13	0–0	6	3	14
McInnis	6–11	0–0	1	9	14
James	7–16	6–6	4	6	21
Williams	0–6	0–0	2	1	0
Battie	1–4	0–0	3	0	2
Ollie	1–4	1–2	0	5	3
Wagner	3–8	0–0	2	1	7
Kapono	7–9	0–0	5	2	19
TOTAL	39–83	17–23	32	29	104

3-Point Goals: 9–17 (Kapono 5–5, McInnis 2–4, Wagner 1–2, James 1–5, Williams 0–1)

Attendance: 17,093

#40

We Will Win

Nate Thurmond's jersey was the first ever retired by the Cavaliers, yet many current fans are completely unaware of what precisely he did to earn the distinction.

Though he was eventually inducted into the Hall of Fame, he never played a full season in Cleveland and only averaged five points per game in wine and gold over the better part of the final two years of his storied career—not exactly the kind of résumé that gets your laundry hung from the rafters. In fact, he was already well past his prime when the Cavs acquired Thurmond in a seemingly ordinary trade with Chicago for Steve Patterson and Eric Fernsten early in the 1975–76 season.

When Thurmond arrived in late November, Cleveland was struggling. After a memorable finish that saw them come within a victory of their first-ever playoff birth the previous spring, the Cavs stumbled to a 6–11 start and appeared to be heading nowhere. Little did the team and its fans know what a difference the thirty-four-year-old veteran from Akron's Central Hower High School would make—and how he would forever alter franchise history.

As soon as Thurmond settled into his role, the Cavs' season made a 180-degree turn. Providing experience off the bench to relieve leading scorer Jim Chones, Thurmond was exactly what Cleveland had been missing. The seventeen-plus minutes he'd play per game were often the key to a Cavs' victory, giving Chones a chance to rest while still providing solid center play.

Cleveland won five of eight before embarking on a West Coast string that began with back-to-back blowout wins over the Lakers and Sonics. But the turning point for the season—and perhaps the franchise itself—came on a December night in Phoenix, Arizona, where the Cavaliers had never won before.

The Suns, 14–9 at the time, were in the midst of their own memorable season that would end with them squaring off with Boston in the NBA Finals.

Behind a red-hot shooting performance, the home team leaped to a ten-point halftime lead and appeared on its way to another easy win over Cleveland. Things looked even worse for the Cavs when coach Bill Fitch was ejected early in the third quarter. Pacing in the locker room like a caged animal, Fitch scribbled the time—9:17 P.M.—and the score—65–54, Phoenix—across the chalkboard. Underneath it, he wrote, "We Will Win." At the other end of the tunnel, the possibility seemed highly unlikely.

Yet sure enough, this was an entirely different Cavaliers team. The visitors roared back to tie the game with a thirty-point third quarter, then rallied from a five-point deficit with fourteen seconds left to send the game to overtime. First, Campy Russell hit a layup to cut the margin to three, then Jim Cleamons picked off a Phoenix pass and Russell drove, scored, and was fouled with six seconds left. His ensuing free throw knotted the contest and sent it to overtime tied at 105.

The suddenly seasoned Cavs didn't miss a beat in the extra session. With Cleveland down one with no time remaining, Austin Carr toed the line for two free throws. He missed the first, but with defeat looming before him, Carr came through to hit the second and send the Cavs to double overtime for the first time in team history. Playing without Russell, who'd fouled out in the first overtime after scoring a game-high twenty-seven points, Cleveland still outlasted the Suns. Cleamons clinched it with a pair of clutch free throws with twelve seconds left, and finally, after a fifty-eight-minute war, the Cavaliers were victorious, 128–124. Fitch's chalkboard prediction, which had seemed so absurd at the time, had come true.

Seven Cleveland players scored in double digits on this night, though Thurmond wasn't one of them. The crafty veteran only scored two points and snagged four rebounds in nineteen minutes, yet he still may have been the MVP. The Cavs had reached .500 for the first time all season and would not dip below it again for two years. Thurmond's mere presence had already paid huge dividends.

It was a franchise-best sixth straight victory, and two nights later in Richfield the string became seven when the Cavs again beat the Lakers. After a seemingly never-ending maturing process, the win in Phoenix proved the Cavaliers were all grown up—and poised to take the city of Cleveland on a miraculous ride.

	1	2	3	4	OT	OT2	
Cavaliers	26	26	30	23	11	12	=128
Suns	29	33	20	23	11	8	=124

CLEVELAND

Player	FG-FGA	FT-FTA	Reb.	Ass.	Pts.
Brewer	6–13	0–0	10	2	12
Smith	11–22	0–2	7	2	22
Chones	9–24	0–1	4	3	18
Cleamons	8–15	2–2	4	5	18
Snyder	4–7	2–2	3	5	10
Carr	6–10	1–2	1	1	13
Thurmond	1–4	0–3	4	1	2
Walker	1–2	0–0	1	2	2
Garratt	2–3	0–0	0	0	4
Russell	9–14	9–10	5	0	27
TOTAL	57–114	14–22	39	21	128

PHOENIX

Player	FG-FGA	FT-FTA	Reb.	Ass.	Pts.
Brickson	9–12	8–9	3	5	26
Perry	5–11	3–4	11	2	13
Adams	9–18	6–8	12	10	24
Van Arsdale	11–14	4–6	3	4	26
Westphal	6–14	3–4	4	9	15
Sobers	4–5	2–2	6	2	10
Shumate	3–8	0–0	6	3	6
Hawthorne	2–4	0–0	1	0	4
TOTAL	49–86	26–33	46	35	124

Attendance: 6,809

PHILADELPHIA 76ERS 138, CAVALIERS 117
MARCH 27, 1981

Joe Tait Day

The fans saw it as a classic confrontation between good and evil, right and wrong, hope and despair. Ironically, for the team—and specifically its ownership—it was just another in a long line of lopsided losses.

If Ted Stepien were purposely trying to destroy the Cavaliers franchise, his actions over his disastrous first season as owner actually would have made sense. He approved ludicrous trades, built an incompetent front office, and waged a personal war with the media. And while Stepien sabotaged a once-beloved franchise, there was a single voice from within the loop pleading for common sense.

That voice belonged to Joe Tait, who had been broadcasting Cavs games on the radio since their first season and had actually become more cherished than the team itself. Tait was like a friendly uncle to the fans, nurturing them through the team's infancy and then personifying the excitement of the miraculous playoff run of 1976. And as the team plummeted into realms of embarrassment that even the expansion days could not match, Tait served as the eyes and ears of a fan base that couldn't bear to witness what was happening. As the team continued to lose and attendance dramatically declined (at one point Stepien and Company decided to offer half-price tickets for all remaining home games), Tait called it as he saw it, often criticizing Stepien and the team on the air.

The clueless Stepien, completely unaware as to the consequences of his buffoonish actions, quickly tired of Tait's back-chat. He sued WWWE, Tait's employer, in response to Tait's criticisms and sought to terminate the team's play-by-play contract with the station. 3W-E gladly forfeited the final two years of its obligation to carry the ratings-challenged Cavs games, yet it meant that Tait, whose contract was with WWWE, was out of a job. What's more, Stepien threatened to fire any Cavaliers employee who associated with Tait and then made good on his promise.

The fans, who had sat almost apathetically through Stepien's front-office shenanigans, were outraged. It was one thing to sabotage the team and ship off favorite players, but to fire Joe Tait was personal. And like foot soldiers catching wind of a coup d'état, the fans mobilized.

Cleveland Mayor George Voinovich declared March 27 "Joe Tait Day." Every media outlet in town hyped the occasion, and the largest crowd in four years piled into the Richfield Coliseum for the final home game in "a season which bordered on science fiction," Bill Nichols wrote. More importantly, they came to witness Tait's 894th and final Cleveland broadcast in what would be the only sellout of Stepien's ludicrous stint as owner.

There was no way, Stepien declared, that 20,000 fans had come to see Tait. "No announcer has a following," he sniveled. "If you want to honor a man, you do it the right way. You have a banquet for him. I think the media created this whole situation. It hurt him and it hurt the Cavs. They came out to see the 76ers, not Joe Tait." At the very least, Stepien was conceding there was no way the home crowd had come out to see the Cavaliers.

But from long before the opening tip until long after the final buzzer, it was clear the game itself meant absolutely nothing to the crowd, which lit up the Coliseum in a way not seen since the Miracle of Richfield days. Tait was bombarded with autograph requests, plaques, and cookies and cakes. Signs reading "Hey Ted, we paid to see Joe" and "Tait is great" and "Let's go Joe" adorned the concourses.

The game itself—a typical twenty-one-point Cleveland loss—was utterly meaningless. In fact, in the waning moments, even the participants paused to appreciate the occasion. A "We Want Joe" chant began near the rafters and echoed down through the Coliseum. It gathered momentum and volume, becoming "a rallying cry for 20,175 trying to preserve an era they saw fading right before their eyes," Tony Grossi wrote in the *Plain Dealer*. Finally, with just over three minutes to play, the ovation became thunderous. Photographers swarmed to press row and snapped pictures of Tait, who tried to stick to business. The 76ers eventually called time out to watch, and even Philly coach Billy Cunningham began applauding the Cavs' outcast broadcaster. Stepien decided he'd seen enough and stormed off down the runway leading from the floor. Fans pummeled him with garbage and food. Once Stepien had gone, Tait rose and waved to his adoring followers, who again erupted.

"It was one of the most memorable nights of my career," Tait said. "It's all been very moving. I'm extremely touched and grateful."

After two more hellish seasons under Stepien, the Cavs persevered and were rescued from oblivion by the Gund brothers in 1983. Tait was immediately rehired. One of the most beloved personalities in Cleveland sports history was back for good.

	1	2	3	4	
76ers	36	35	31	36	=138
Cavaliers	24	30	27	36	=117

PHILADELPHIA

Player	FG-FGA	FT-FTA	Reb.	Ass.	Pts.
Erving	8–12	5–5	7	3	21
C. Jones	3–6	0–0	6	2	6
Dawkins	8–11	4–7	7	0	20
Cheeks	3–9	1–1	2	8	7
Hollins	5–6	0–0	0	3	10
B. Jones	5–8	5–7	9	3	15
Toney	8–11	8–15	2	7	24
Mix	5–8	1–3	6	1	11
Richardson	4–5	6–7	5	1	14
Johnson	1–3	2–2	3	1	4
Cureton	3–3	0–0	0	0	6
TOTAL	53–82	32–47	47	29	138

CLEVELAND

Player	FG-FGA	FT-FTA	Reb.	Ass.	Pts.
Carr	11–15	2–2	10	2	24
Mitchell	14–23	2–2	3	1	30
Laimbeer	2–8	0–0	3	2	4
Phegley	5–14	1–2	3	2	11
Bratz	2–10	2–2	0	10	8
Huston	1–1	0–0	0	0	2
Washington	9–19	1–2	12	3	19
Jordan	1–6	0–0	3	1	2
Smith	4–10	5–6	2	3	13
Calvin	2–3	0–0	0	2	4
TOTAL	51–109	13–16	36	26	117

Attendance: 20,175

CAVALIERS 113, SEATTLE SUPERSONICS 107
NOVEMBER 12, 1972

Lenny's Return

At the dawn of the Cavaliers' third season, Lenny Wilkens was just another respectable player in the NBA. In another two decades, his name would signify an era in franchise history.

The soft-spoken, intelligent point guard from Brooklyn had already enjoyed a marvelous career when he landed in Cleveland as part of a trade for guard Butch Beard just before the 1972–73 campaign began. Though his Hall of Fame career would later become entwined with the Cavaliers, Wilkens was anything but happy with the transaction. He'd spent the previous three seasons as a player/coach in Seattle, winning forty-seven games the year before. But when Sonics' owner Sam Schulman replaced Wilkens as coach with Tom Nissalke (who would also wind up coaching in Cleveland in the decade to come), he also decided Wilkens was expendable as a player. Wilkens, who was comfortable and happy in Seattle, refused to report to Cleveland and threatened to retire. Many Seattle fans were also outraged, and several season-ticket holders canceled their orders.

When Wilkens finally joined the Cavs, they were 0–7. Interestingly, two weeks later, they would play in Seattle. And a standing-room-only crowd of better than 13,000—the second-largest in Seattle history—filed into the Seattle Center Coliseum primarily to voice displeasure over the Sonics' treatment of Wilkens. The Seattle front office tried to preempt public opinion, hanging saccharine signs throughout the arena supporting the suddenly struggling team and its beleaguered new coach. But as soon as the doors opened, the fans removed those signs and replaced them with banners supporting Wilkens. The tone was set before the opening tip. Whenever Wilkens or Barry Clemens, also dealt away by Seattle in a controversial trade to Cleveland in the off-season, made a shot in warm-ups, the crowd roared. "It was like a home game for us," Cavs' forward John Johnson said afterward.

Though the Cavs had lost four straight, most recently a thirty-point shellacking in Los Angeles two nights before, they looked like the better team from the outset. They roared to a nine-point lead after one period that swelled to a 60–46 advantage at the half. And with his former fans cheering him on and booing his old team, Wilkens played one of the finest games of his life, scoring twenty-two points while adding nine assists and nine rebounds. And when the Sonics closed to within four points in the final minute, Johnson hit a pair of free throws and Austin Carr added a clinching bucket to salt away a 113–107 victory—the seventh straight defeat for the Sonics. Without Wilkens to guide them, the Sonics would lose fifty-six games in 1972–73—a twenty-one-game turnaround from the previous season. "It was a pressure game for Lenny and, in fact, for all the guys," Bill Fitch said. "They all came through. It was a game a bunch of young guys will never forget."

And neither would the crowd. Though in the previous decade Seattle had put itself on the map by hosting the World's Fair and, briefly, a Major League Baseball team, "none drew more excitement than Lenny Wilkens' homecoming," the *Plain Dealer* declared.

Wilkens would play two seasons with the Cavaliers, providing the steady, experienced hand the team desperately needed as it matured into a playoff contender. After retiring as a player in 1975, Wilkens began his coaching career in earnest, returning to Seattle to lead the Sonics for eight seasons and capture the franchise's only title in 1979. Perhaps appropriately, he followed up his Seattle tenure with a return to Cleveland, where between 1986 and 1993 he became the most successful coach in Cavalier history.

Inducted into the Hall of Fame as a player in 1989, Wilkens would go on to become the all-time winningest coach, tallying 1,332 victories in thirty-two seasons. Both as a player and a coach, he may have been the most successful individual to ever grace either franchise. And neither would forget the November night when his destiny crossed theirs.

	1	2	3	4	
Cavaliers	33	27	31	22	=113
SuperSonics	24	22	32	29	=107

CLEVELAND

Player	FG	FT-FTA	Pts.
Davis	7	6–6	20
Johnson	6	7–7	19
Patterson	1	6–10	8
Carr	8	6–7	22
Wilkens	7	8–10	22
Cleamons	1	2–2	4
Clemens	0	0–0	0
Smith	1	0–0	2
Warner	7	0–0	14
Warren	1	0–0	2
Rule	0	0–0	0
TOTAL	39	35–42	113

SEATTLE

Player	FG	FT-FTA	Pts.
Brisker	6	2–2	14
Haywood	12	4–4	28
Fox	0	3–6	3
Snyder	3	2–2	8
Winfield	6	3–5	15
Beard	4	8–11	16
Brown	5	4–4	14
McDaniels	1	0–0	2
McIntosh	3	0–0	6
Wright	0	1–3	1
TOTAL	40	27–37	107

Attendance: 13,174

CAVALIERS 86, INDIANA PACERS 77
APRIL 27, 1998

A Gund-Raising Event

For as much comparable excitement that the construction and opening of Cleveland's two shining new sports complexes garnered in 1994, there couldn't have been a greater difference in the immediate impact the buildings made on their respective teams.

Jacobs Field instantly carried the downtrodden Indians into the upper echelon of Major League Baseball. After going forty-one years without a postseason appearance, the Tribe reached the playoffs five straight times, twice making the World Series. Meanwhile, across Eagle Avenue, the Cavs' fortunes stayed exactly the same at Gund Arena—and arguably got worse. The Cavaliers reached the postseason three times in their first four seasons at the new facility just as they'd done in the last four seasons at the Richfield Coliseum. But while the Cavs had enjoyed modest postseason success in Richfield, they'd seen none on their return to downtown.

As the team prepared to host the favored Indiana Pacers for Game Three of their best-of-five first-round series in the 1998 playoffs, it found itself trying to rectify its home-court disadvantage. The Cavs hadn't won a home postseason game in five years, dropping seven straight, while losing a whopping fifteen of their previous sixteen overall playoff games. Though the Gund may have been aesthetically pleasing, it wasn't the kind of place at which opposing teams feared playing. One *Plain Dealer* columnist described it as the "home of the ringing cell phone that disturbs the sleep of the swells in the loges." Not surprisingly, the late-arriving crowd for Game Three did not fill the arena.

For their part, the Cavs had done little to garner excitement, dropping the first two games in Indianapolis and squandering a seventeen-point lead in Game Two. And with a sweep in their sights, the Pacers leaped to a nine-point lead in the first quarter. But one Cavalier wasn't about to let the team slip quietly into the off-season. Forward Shawn Kemp had already had a terrific series, scoring fifty-two points in the first two games, and with the season's end beckoning, Kemp rose to the occasion. He sparked the Cavs to a two-point halftime lead, continually yelling at and urging his teammates. Early in the third quarter, Kemp dove after a loose ball, inspiring both the Cavs players and the crowd, which became louder and louder as the game went on. The cell phones were off and nobody was sleeping.

With Cleveland rookie guard Brevin Knight containing Indiana veteran Mark Jackson, the Cavs again rallied from a five-point deficit late in the third quarter. After holding Indiana without a field goal for more than six minutes, they took a lead into the fourth quarter. When the Pacers cut the margin to two with four minutes to play, Cleveland outscored the visitors 11–4 down the stretch, sparked by a key eighteen-footer by Knight which swung momentum back to the Cavs.

When Kemp hit the game-clinching shot with twenty-nine seconds left, he broke into an impromptu victory dance at midcourt. Teammate Cedric Henderson laid the basketball on the ground beside him and Kemp put his foot on it in triumph. "That," Kemp said later, "is what you call feeling good out there." Coach Mike Fratello surmised that Kemp "simply did not want to go home tonight." The powerful postman scored thirty-one points and ripped down seven rebounds in what would prove to be the only postseason victory in his short but electric tenure in Cleveland.

The final was 86–77, the Cavs' first-ever playoff win at Gund Arena. Unfortunately, while the victory snapped a frustrating skid, it didn't change the team's postseason fortunes. Three nights later, Indiana eliminated Cleveland, and eight more years would elapse before the Cavs would win another post-season contest.

	1	2	3	4	
Pacers	27	15	19	16	=77
Cavaliers	22	22	21	21	=86

INDIANA

Player	FG-FGA	FT-FTA	Reb.	Ass.	Pts.
Mullin	2–5	1–1	1	0	6
D. Davis	4–5	3–4	9	0	11
Smits	11–17	4–4	8	1	26
Jackson	1–6	1–2	1	17	3
Miller	7–16	2–2	2	3	18
A. Davis	0–4	2–2	3	0	2
Rose	3–10	0–0	1	3	7
McKey	2–5	0–0	2	0	4
Best	0–1	0–0	2	1	0
TOTAL	30–69	13–15	29	25	77

3-Point Goals: 4–17 (Miller 2–8, Mullin 1–3, Rose 1–3, Jackson 0–3)

CLEVELAND

Player	FG-FGA	FT-FTA	Reb.	Ass.	Pts.
Henderson	4–9	1–3	6	5	9
Kemp	11–21	9–10	7	2	31
Ilgauskas	5–12	3–8	5	0	13
Knight	4–8	3–6	7	5	11
Person	2–5	2–2	2	4	7
Anderson	2–4	7–8	5	5	11
Potapenko	2–4	0–0	4	0	4
Sura	0–1	0–0	0	0	0
TOTAL	30–64	25–37	36	21	86

3-Point Goals: 1–5 (Person 1–4, Sura 0–1)

Attendance: 17,495

CAVALIERS 110, BOSTON CELTICS 105
FEBRUARY 6, 1973

Green With Envy

As the toddling Cavaliers neared the conclusion of their third season, there was a very clear beacon of success they—and every other NBA team—were trying to follow and emulate. That was the shimmering jewel of the NBA's relatively brief history: the Boston Celtics.

As the 1970s began, the Celtics had already captured eleven NBA titles dating back to 1957, turning storied Boston Garden into a museum, highlighting the achievements of legendary players like Bob Cousy, Bill Russell, K. C. Jones, Tom Heinsohn, Sam Jones, Bailey Howell, Dave Cowens, and John Havlicek. Yet even with so much glory to contend with, the 1972–73 Celtics would distinguish themselves as the finest team in franchise history.

With Havlicek, Cowens, and pesky guard Jo Jo White all averaging nearly twenty points per game, Boston tore through the schedule, winning its first ten games and twenty-six of its first twenty-nine. The Celtics marched into an early February match at Cleveland Arena with a 43–10 mark, an obvious favorite over the 19–35 Cavaliers, who had lost three straight and were already well out of the playoff hunt. What's more, Boston had handled Cleveland convincingly in their previous four matches that season, winning by an average of nearly nineteen points per contest.

But something was different on this night. True, Havlicek was out with a knee injury, but the Cavs came in dinged up as well. Most notably, Lenny Wilkens, the team's second-best scorer, was iffy with an injured tendon in his foot. He decided to give it a shot and wound up turning an ankle late in the first half. Yet Wilkens fought his way through the pain as the still-outmanned Cavs finally stood up to the mighty Celtics.

Cleveland took a four-point lead into the second quarter, but Boston scratched back and soared to a 59–55 lead early in the third. With Havlicek out, forward Don Nelson picked up the slack, tripling his season average with thirty points. But on the other end of the floor, another player also rose to the occasion. Austin Carr, who had been struggling in recent weeks, exploded for twenty-eight points and followed Wilkens's lead as Cleveland ripped off a 34–15 run to take an 89–74 lead midway through the fourth quarter. The modest crowd of 4,000-plus then willed the team to hang on as White led a furious charge to cut the margin to three in the final seconds before the Cavs sealed the win.

Some were quick to point out that All-Star Havlicek hadn't played. But the Celtics knew that wasn't the difference. "We got beat, that's all," Heinsohn admitted. "We didn't play good defense and Cleveland did. The Cavaliers have played good games when Havlicek played. Give 'em credit. They played well." The real difference was battered Lenny Wilkens, who turned in one of the finest performances of his career as he scored thirty-one points, dished out eleven assists, and ripped down nine rebounds. He was, the Celtics felt, exactly what the inexperienced Cavaliers needed. "When they got Lenny," Nelson said, "that was it. They were coming on before and now they're a good ball club." Celtics' center Paul Silas agreed: "Cleveland already had the makings of a good team, but with Wilkens they're on their way."

And following the stunning loss in Cleveland, the Celtics were on their way. From that point on, Boston would win twenty-five of its final twenty-eight games and come within one victory of tying the league record for triumphs in a season. As it was, the 68–14 record still stands as the finest in Celtic history and the fourth best in NBA history.

But for one moment, the mighty Celtics were envious of the rag-tag Cleveland Cavaliers.

	1	2	3	4	
Celtics	24	26	24	31	=105
Cavaliers	28	23	38	21	=110

BOSTON

Player	FG-FGA	FT-FTA	Reb.	Ass.	Pts.
Chaney	7–12	0–0	8	4	14
Cowens	7–14	1–2	14	4	15
Kuberski	1–6	0–0	3	0	2
Nelson	12–24	6–7	7	2	30
Finkel	0–0	0–0	0	1	0
Sanders	1–2	0–0	0	0	2
Silas	4–12	5–6	16	8	13
Westphal	0–2	0–0	0	0	0
White	11–24	5–7	6	7	27
Williams	1–6	0–0	1	2	2
TOTAL	44–102	17–22	55	28	105

CLEVELAND

Player	FG-FGA	FT-FTA	Reb.	Ass.	Pts.
Carr	11–23	6–8	9	3	28
Cleamons	1–3	0–0	2	5	2
Clemens	3–8	0–0	2	2	6
Davis	3–10	1–2	5	1	7
Johnson	7–17	5–6	4	3	19
Roberson	5–11	1–3	5	2	11
Smith	0–2	0–0	1	2	0
Warner	2–4	2–3	8	2	6
Wilkens	11–18	9–10	9	11	31
Patterson	0–2	0–0	0	0	0
TOTAL	43–98	24–32	45	31	110

Attendance: 4,023

CAVALIERS 80, DETROIT PISTONS 79
JANUARY 27, 1989

Friday Night Fights

As the Cavaliers gradually improved during their much-ballyhooed rebuilding process in the late 1980s, they'd garnered respect around the league. They'd become a force to be dealt with in 1987–88, going from a fifty-one-loss season to taking Michael Jordan and the Bulls to the deciding game in a first-round playoff series. And as the 1988–89 campaign neared its midpoint, they'd commanded attention with a 30–8 start and a four-game lead in the Central Division over the defending conference champion Detroit Pistons.

But along with that new respect came an undesired reputation: the friendly, sportsmanlike Cavs were soft.

Though the players and coaches dismissed it as ridiculous, noting that you couldn't have the kind of success Cleveland had enjoyed without intestinal fortitude. Still, the perception persevered—until the Cavaliers smothered it on a Friday night in Auburn Hills, Michigan.

The host Pistons had reason to be grumpy. After blowing a three-games-to-two lead to the Lakers in the '88 Finals, they'd spent most of the 1988–89 season eating the Cavaliers' dust. After getting blasted in Cleveland a month earlier, their burgeoning "Bad Boy" image hung in the balance—and they intended to do something about it. "It will be a physical game," Cavs' coach Lenny Wilkens said the day before. "They like to hold and grab and bang and they'll be pumped up." He had no idea.

Much as they'd done in their previous meeting, the Cavs gained the upper hand, building a nine-point halftime lead. The margin swelled to sixteen points early in the third quarter when the frustrated Pistons made their move. In a scramble for a loose ball, Detroit designated troublemaker Bill Laimbeer bear-hugged the Cavs' Brad Daugherty. Daugherty, fully expecting the Pistons' shenanigans, swung his arms violently to break free and struck Laimbeer in the process. Pistons' guard Isaiah Thomas then grabbed Daugherty from behind as Laimbeer landed a punch on Daugherty's face.

The sellout Palace crowd rose to its feet, anticipating another Piston brawl. But the officials took control, ejecting both Laimbeer and Daugherty. Each would be suspended for one game and fined $5,000. "I'm not really sure if they tried to start something on purpose or not," Daugherty said later. "Maybe they did, maybe they didn't." Either way, Laimbeer's cheap shot caused Daugherty no pain. "Not at all," he said. "Laimbeer punches like a girl." Yet it would prove to cause the Cavs some discomfort. Since to that point Laimbeer had hit just one of seven shots for two points with four rebounds, while Daugherty had scored fourteen points to go along with seven rebounds and four assists, it seemed Laimbeer's assault wasn't entirely impulsive.

A few minutes later, forward Rick Mahorn, another Piston thug, picked a fight with Cavs' leading rebounder Larry Nance, but Wilkens jumped between them to break it up before any punches were thrown. "We got the lead and they wanted to knock us around," said Cavs' point guard Mark Price. "You don't like to get into those sorts of situations, but we're not going to back down from them, either."

"No class," grumbled Cavs' general manager Wayne Embry. "Neither one of them [Laimbeer or Mahorn] has any class. There is no place in the game for what those two did."

When the dust settled, the crowd was hostile, the Pistons were fired up, and the Cavs were shorthanded. Detroit took advantage, holding Cleveland without a field goal for seven minutes while embarking on a 14–0 run to tie the contest with less than four minutes left.

Though they'd taken it on the chin—both literally and figuratively—the Cavs refused to surrender. Price hit a ten-foot jumper to get the lead back, then connected on two critical free throws with fifty-one seconds remaining to put Cleveland up 80–77. Thomas responded with a fifteen-foot jump shot to cut the lead to one with twenty-seven ticks left, then Price missed a three-pointer, giving Detroit one last chance for victory. But Thomas missed from eighteen feet with six seconds left, then after a wild scramble for the rebound, his desperation shot from half court just missed as the buzzer sounded. The Cavs had stood up to the bullies in their own garage and come away with an incredibly satisfying victory, snapping a string of seven straight road defeats to the Pistons.

"For some reason, people around the league think we aren't going to take the sort of crap the Pistons deal out," Daugherty said. "Well, we won't, and now they know we won't." With one gritty victory, as Burt Graeff wrote in the *Plain Dealer*, the Cavs "forever ruined the finesse, nice-guy image that had dogged them for most of the last three seasons." And in so doing, they announced to the rest of the league they wouldn't back down to anyone—not even the Bad Boys.

	1	2	3	4	
Cavaliers	27	21	22	10	=80
Pistons	21	18	18	22	=79

CLEVELAND

Player	FG-FGA	FT-FTA	Reb.	Ass.	Pts.
Nance	5–13	1–1	9	3	11
Sanders	3–8	2–4	4	2	8
Daugherty	7–8	0–0	7	4	14
Price	9–17	4–4	1	3	22
Harper	4–11	2–2	5	9	10
Williams	3–7	6–7	5	0	12
Ehlo	0–2	0–0	3	1	0
Dudley	1–1	1–1	4	0	3
Valentine	0–0	0–2	0	1	0
Rollins	0–3	0–0	1	0	0
TOTAL	32–70	16–21	39	23	80

3-Point Goals: 0–2 (Price 0–1, Harper 0–1)

DETROIT

Player	FG-FGA	FT-FTA	Reb.	Ass.	Pts.
Dantley	2–11	7–9	5	1	11
Salley	3–5	0–0	6	0	6
Laimbeer	1–7	0–0	4	0	2
Johnson	10–22	2–3	2	1	22
Thomas	10–22	2–3	7	5	22
Mahorn	0–1	0–0	2	0	0
Rodman	4–7	0–2	17	2	8
Williams	0–0	0–0	0	0	0
Edwards	3–11	2–3	6	1	8
TOTAL	33–86	13–20	49	10	79

3-Point Goals: 0–2 (Thomas 0–2)

Attendance: 21,454

CAVALIERS 86, DETROIT PISTONS 84

MAY 17, 2006

A Learning Experience

It was supposed to be a learning experience, nothing more. The upstart Cavaliers were just supposed to pop into the NBA playoffs, get third-year superstar LeBron James some experience, and then come back the following year with hopes of actually making some noise.

When Cleveland knocked off a veteran Washington team in the first round, few took notice. With the defending conference champion Detroit Pistons waiting in the wings for the Eastern Conference semifinals, most figured the Cavs would be tidily excused in the next round. After all, Detroit had won a league-best sixty-four games during the season, secured the Central Division by a comfortable fourteen games over Cleveland, and swept past the Cavs in three of their four meetings, winning by an average of sixteen points per game. And, to no one's surprise, the Pistons coasted to easy victories in the first two games to take command of a series it appeared they wouldn't even have to break a sweat for.

Suddenly, the untested Cavaliers stood tall, pulling out clutch victories in Games Three and Four at Quicken Loans Arena to send the series back to Detroit knotted at two games apiece. And they'd clawed back without third-leading scorer Larry Hughes, who missed both games while attending the funeral of his younger brother, who'd died of heart failure. Hughes would also miss the fifth game as his teammates would once again have to step up to account for the sixteen points, five rebounds, and four assists missing from the lineup.

Though they'd never won three straight playoff games in franchise history, the Cavs seemed to own the game from the opening tip. They rolled to a five-point halftime lead which swelled to a ten-point advantage in the third. But the Pistons then showed the resolve that had propelled them to the NBA Finals each of the previous two years, scraping back to tie the game at sixty-six.

The teams battled through a titanic fourth quarter, with momentum swinging back and forth like a giant pendulum. When the Cavs took a lead into the final two minutes, Detroit forward Antonio McDyess tied the contest at eighty-four with 1:20 left. The Pistons then had a golden opportunity to take the lead, but forward Ben Wallace missed a pair of free throws with forty seconds remaining. Now the Cavs were in the driver's seat and were set to pull off the play of the game.

Forwards Drew Gooden and Donyell Marshall set a double pick for James, who scooted around Wallace as Marshall popped out to the three-point arc and Gooden rolled to the basket. James patiently waited for Gooden to slide open along the baseline, then fired a dart of a pass to him underneath the basket. Gooden laid the ball through the iron with twenty-seven seconds left to give the Cavs the lead. But they weren't out of the woods yet.

It was Marshall's turn to play hero next, as he blocked a soft Tayshaun Prince shot in the lane—the Cavs' tenth blocked shot of the night. Detroit guard Lindsey Hunter regained possession and missed a putback attempt, and after a wild scramble that ended with the ball caroming out of bounds, Detroit was awarded possession with 1.8 ticks showing. But James and Marshall double-teamed guard Rich Hamilton after he received the in-bound pass and Hamilton lost control of the ball as time expired. The Cavs' six-game losing streak in Detroit was history, and they were now one victory away from the conference finals for the first time in fourteen years.

Though the Pistons would rally to win the next two games and advance, the unassuming Cavaliers had turned their innocent little learning experience into something not to be forgotten.

	1	2	3	4	
Cavaliers	20	30	18	18	=86
Pistons	20	25	21	18	=84

CLEVELAND

Player	FG-FGA	FT-FTA	Reb.	Ass.	Pts.
James	13–30	5–7	5	5	32
Gooden	2–5	0–0	4	1	4
Ilgauskas	6–13	2–2	10	1	14
Murray	2–10	4–6	2	0	8
Snow	0–5	0–0	3	7	0
Marshall	5–9	2–2	13	0	14
Varejao	0–4	6–8	3	0	6
Jones	3–5	0–1	3	1	8
Newble	0–0	0–0	1	0	0
TOTAL	31–81	19–26	44	15	86

3-Point Goals: 5–13 (Jones 2–4, Marshall 2–4, James 1–4, Murray 0–1)

DETROIT

Player	FG-FGA	FT-FTA	Reb.	Ass.	Pts.
Prince	7–13	6–6	8	2	21
R. Wallace	5–9	0–0	9	1	10
B. Wallace	4–9	0–7	13	1	8
Hamilton	5–16	5–7	1	3	15
Billups	6–16	4–4	3	5	17
Hunter	0–2	0–0	2	3	0
McDyess	5–9	1–2	11	1	11
Evans	0–1	2–2	0	0	2
TOTAL	32–75	18–28	47	16	84

3-Point Goals: 2–10 (Prince 1–1, Billups 1–6, Hamilton 0–1, Hunter 0–1, R. Wallace 0–1)

Attendance: 22,076

CAVALIERS 112, BOSTON CELTICS 108
JANUARY 26, 1972

Basketball's Haunted House

It was the quintessential haunted house of professional basketball, where the ghosts of glorious achievements of yesterday circled through the rafters and awed all visitors. Nearly twice as old as the NBA itself, Boston Garden had been the home of fifteen world-title teams by the early 1970s—eleven from the Celtics and four by the National Hockey League's Bruins, who would capture a fifth Stanley Cup in 1972. From the retired jerseys dangling above the rickety, unreliable parquet floor beneath, Boston Garden was not only a spooky place but perhaps the greatest example of home-field advantage in professional sports.

By contrast, midway through their second year of existence, the Cleveland Cavaliers were still the league's horror show. Their brief history consisted primarily of ugly losses—more than 100 in the franchise's first sixteen months of existence. Accordingly, the fledging Cavs had just a 7–55 all-time road record as their second January came to a close. After a relatively promising start to the season, Cleveland rung in 1972 with an eleven-game losing streak and brought a 15–35 record into the Garden to face the 34–17 Celtics, who had won five of their last six and were looking to expand their lead over rival New York in the Atlantic Division. It was perhaps the worst time for a trip to Boston.

So it came as no surprise when the Celtics sprinted to a sixteen-point third-quarter lead before a somewhat bored and miniscule Garden crowd. Legendary forward John Havlicek was hot, hitting thirteen shots and scoring twenty-seven points while future Hall-of-Famers Dave Cowens and Don Nelson were also dominant down low as the Celtics were coasting toward victory. But somehow, the Cavaliers got on a roll. They cut the margin to six going into the fourth quarter, when a suddenly revved-up offense exploded for thirty-six points, giving them a total of sixty-six in the second half alone.

Forward Dave Sorensen, who would score twenty points in his first professional start, tipped in a Cleveland miss to tie the contest with four minutes to play. Moments later rookie Austin Carr drilled a short jumper to give the Cavaliers a lead they would not relinquish.

When Boston inched closer in the waning minutes, Cleveland center Walt Wesley, one of the few proven veterans on a team overflowing with youngsters and castoffs, scored six points in the final 1:11—a huge dunk and four critical free throws. And when the final buzzer sounded, the Cavaliers had captured their first-ever victory in storied Boston Garden.

Not surprisingly, relatively few Cleveland wins would follow in the next twenty-three years the Celtics occupied the Garden. It would be almost three years before they would capture their second, and the Cavs would finish with just a 12–48 record there. Between 1978 and 1988, the Cavs lost twenty-seven straight road games to Boston, and only twice in a quarter-century did they win more than one regular-season game in Boston in a season. Of the eight playoff games it played at Boston Garden, Cleveland lost seven, though five were by five points or fewer—perhaps indicative of the subtle advantage the building created for the home team.

But for one memorable night in 1972, the overmatched Cavs conquered sports' ultimate haunted house.

	1	2	3	4	
Cavaliers	23	23	30	36	=112
Celtics	30	30	22	26	=108

CLEVELAND

Player	FG	FT-FTA	Pts.
Johnson	9	4–4	22
Sorensen	8	4–6	20
Roberson	4	5–6	13
Beard	7	9–14	23
Carr	7	2–2	16
B. Smith	3	0–0	6
Warren	0	0–0	0
Howard	1	0–0	2
Wesley	1	4–5	6
Washington	1	2–2	4
TOTAL	41	30–39	112

BOSTON

Player	FG	FT-FTA	Pts.
Havlicek	13	1–1	27
Sanders	2	2–3	6
Cowens	8	2–3	18
White	9	2–5	20
Chaney	7	0–0	14
Nelson	5	5–5	15
Williams	3	0–1	6
Kuberski	1	0–0	2
Finkel	0	0–0	0
Morgan	0	0–0	0
TOTAL	48	12–18	108

Attendance: 3,016

#32

CAVALIERS 108, CHICAGO BULLS 105 (OT)
MAY 5, 1989

Backs to the Wall

The Cavaliers had spent most of the 1988–89 season deluging their opponents with their superior talent and a winning attitude. Now, after a few cruel twists of fate, they were just trying to keep their heads above water.

After surrendering what once seemed like a certain Central Division title, the Cavs limped into the playoffs with four key players nursing injuries. "If it wasn't for bad luck," Mark Price said that week, "seems like we'd have no luck at all." Still, most figured Cleveland would coast through the first round anyway, since it was paired with the Chicago Bulls, whom the Cavs had defeated all six times they'd played in the regular season. Yet for some reason, Bulls' superstar Michael Jordan was profoundly confident heading into the series—so much so that he predicted Chicago would upset Cleveland in four games.

With Price on the sideline with a pulled groin and sprained wrist, the lethargic Cavs were stunned at Richfield Coliseum in Game One, then after rebounding to win the second game, were overwhelmed at Chicago Stadium in Game Three. The Bulls needed just one more win on their home court to make Jordan's prediction reality. With Price, Brad Daugherty (foot), Larry Nance (ankle), and Craig Ehlo (ankle) all hobbling and the Cavs' twelve-year road playoff losing streak hovering at fourteen games, the clock appeared ready to strike midnight on the Cavs' Cinderella season. Their slump may have been easily explained and justified, but as the *Plain Dealer*'s Bill Livingston wrote, "all Cleveland sees is a house of cards tumbling down."

Yet with their backs to the wall, the Cavs didn't allow the Bulls to surge to comfortable early leads as they had in the first three games. Game Four would be tied on thirty-four occasions and the lead would change hands thirteen times. Cleveland led by one at the intermission, then the battered Price caught fire, hitting four straight jumpers to start the second half, sparking a fourteen-point third-quarter explosion for the tiny guard who had missed twenty-six of thirty-three shots in his last two games of the series. But the Bulls fought back to take a lead into the fourth quarter and were poised to clinch the game when Jordan was sent to the free-throw line with the Bulls up one with nine seconds left. Jordan, who had already scored forty-eight points on the night and a whopping 153 in the series, made the first but missed the second, leaving the window of opportunity open just a crack for the Cavaliers.

On their ensuing possession, Daugherty was fouled and had a chance to tie the game with four seconds showing. A few hours before, the beefy center from North Carolina was perhaps the last player the Cavs wanted to see in this situation. He was a miserable eight for twenty-one from the free-throw stripe in the series. But after working with free-throw maestro Mark Price at a morning shoot-around, Daugherty's fortunes had changed dramatically. He would make eleven of twelve charity shots for the night—and calmly knocked down the biggest two of his career to tie the contest and send it to overtime. "All that was going through my mind was seeing that ball go through the bottom of the net," Daugherty said. "I was going to make them. No doubt about it."

The beleaguered Cavs dug deep and took charge in the extra session, ripping off six straight points and holding Jordan to a single digit before he fouled out with a minute left. But even with Jordan gone, the Bulls didn't quit. They cut the margin to 107–105, then Cavs' guard Ron Harper hit a clutch foul shot, though he missed another that would have iced the contest with eight seconds left. The Bulls had two clear three-point shots in the waning moments, but both were off the mark, and the Cavs survived to fight another day with perhaps the grittiest victory in franchise history.

"This was the Cavaliers team that failed to show for much of the first three games of this surprisingly difficult series," Bob Kravitz wrote in the *Plain Dealer,* "a Cavaliers team with singularity of purpose, guts, and character."

	1	2	3	4	OT	
Cavaliers	23	26	25	25	9	=108
Bulls	22	26	28	23	6	=105

CLEVELAND

Player	FG-FGA	FT-FTA	Reb.	Ass.	Pts.
Williams	4–8	0–0	5	2	8
Nance	11–17	5–10	9	3	27
Daugherty	2–10	11–12	17	1	15
Harper	6–12	5–6	5	4	17
Price	8–13	6–7	3	7	24
Rollins	1–2	0–0	2	0	2
Valentine	0–2	0–0	1	0	0
Ehlo	0–6	1–2	1	3	1
Dudley	0–1	0–0	0	0	0
Sanders	6–11	2–3	7	0	14
TOTAL	38–82	30–40	50	20	108

3-Point Goals: 2–4 (Price 2–2, Ehlo 0–2)

CHICAGO

Player	FG-FGA	FT-FTA	Reb.	Ass.	Pts.
Pippen	5–12	3–4	8	5	15
Grant	3–7	1–4	16	3	7
Cartwright	5–10	2–3	13	0	12
Hodges	2–8	2–2	2	5	6
Jordan	14–28	22–27	3	4	50
Sellers	3–6	2–2	3	0	8
Paxson	0–1	0–0	0	3	0
Corzine	2–5	1–1	1	1	5
Vincent	1–6	0–0	0	3	2
Davis	0–1	0–0	1	0	0
TOTAL	35–84	33–43	47	24	105

3-Point Goals: 2–9 (Pippen 2–4, Jordan 0–1, Davis 0–1, Hodges 0–3)

Attendance: 18,264

CAVALIERS 113, UTAH JAZZ 112
DECEMBER 23, 1991

Yes, Virginia . . .

In the five seasons since he'd joined the Cavaliers, guard Craig Ehlo had gone from the very personification of obscurity to one of the best clutch players in the NBA. A native of Lubbock, Texas, and a solid but not spectacular player at Washington State, he'd come to Cleveland almost by accident. While playing with the Mississippi Coast Jets of the Continental Basketball Association in January 1987, Ehlo signed a ten-day contract with Cleveland when the Cavs desperately needed a warm body to play guard after Mark Price underwent an emergency appendectomy midway through his rookie season.

Ehlo's versatility and work ethic gradually earned him more and more playing time, and by the following season, he was Cleveland's most valuable bench player. Then, when Ron Harper was traded away early in the 1989–90 season, Ehlo picked up the slack in the backcourt, dramatically increasing his playing time and nearly doubling his scoring average. And he always seemed to come up big when the Cavs needed it most.

But the greatest moment of Ehlo's journeyman career came on an otherwise ordinary Monday night just before Christmas 1991. The crisp Cavs were facing the equally efficient Utah Jazz in what would become a classic game at Richfield Coliseum. The teams matched one another basket for basket for much of the game, with neither leading by more than eight points. The Cavs finally appeared to have victory in their grasp, building a 107–102 lead with 1:32 to play, but Utah ripped off six straight points to take a one-point advantage in the waning seconds.

Then, with 9.7 seconds left, Price drilled a three-point shot to put Cleveland up 110–108 and the Coliseum crowd once again could taste triumph. But again, the Jazz wouldn't quit. Wily guard John Stockton quickly drove into the lane and hit a running ten-footer to tie the contest with 2.8 ticks on the clock. Then the Cavs made two crushing mistakes that appeared to cost them the game.

Forward Henry James grabbed the ball just after it went through the hoop following Stockton's shot and, thinking there was less than a second remaining, rifled a pass the length of the court, hoping to hit Hot Rod Williams for a game-winning layup. But the ball sailed over Williams and out of bounds along the opposite baseline—giving the ball back to Utah beneath the hoop where James had launched the ball. Larry Nance then lost track of Utah forward Blue Edwards on the ensuing inbound play and Edwards took the pass and laid the ball in the hoop to give the Jazz a 112–110 lead with 1.3 seconds left. The Cavaliers, after an incredible seesaw sequence, took time and frantically drew up their last-gasp play. *"You've heard of the Miracle of 34th Street,"* Joe Tait told his radio audience, *"how about the Miracle of Streetsboro Road? They're going to need one."*

Ehlo would inbound near midcourt. He had three options on the play, and all three were covered. Seeing Ehlo was stuck, Brad Daugherty stepped up off the post and Ehlo flipped him the ball. "I knew if I threw to him, I would get it back," Ehlo said. "I had my mind focused on taking that shot. I had to go right back up with it." As Utah's Jeff Malone left Ehlo to double-team Daugherty, the Cavs' center tossed the basketball back to Ehlo, who had stepped inbounds and planted his feet just outside the three-point arc. In one fluid motion, Ehlo caught the ball and leaped upward, releasing the shot just before the clock hit zero.

The basketball exploded through the net as the buzzer sounded, sending the previously hushed crowd of 16,181 into hysterics. Ehlo's teammates swarmed to him along the sideline. Price, seven inches shorter, lifted Ehlo off the ground. Daugherty hugged him so hard Ehlo started to get light-headed. It was a moment of jubilation that would be depicted not only on the cover of the team's media guide the following year, but it would be forever frozen in Cavs' history.

But perhaps those who remember the play best were the ones who didn't see it. Joe Tait's radio call floated into the holiday air and became instant legend: *"Ehlo looking, looking . . . fires to Daugherty, back to Ehlo, the three in the air. . . . IT'S GOOD! HE WON IT! Ehlo hit a three-pointer on the sideline at the buzzer! Yes, Virginia, there is a Santa Claus, and he comes from Lubbock, Texas!"*

It marked the second time in three years Ehlo had defeated Utah with a three-pointer at the buzzer, but the umpteenth time he'd saved the day when the chips were down. "If anybody can make it, Craig can," Nance said. "He's that type of guy."

And in so doing, much like Saint Nick himself, Craig Ehlo ensured a very merry Christmas for the Cavs and their fans.

	1	2	3	4	
Jazz	29	26	26	31	=112
Cavaliers	26	30	28	29	=113

UTAH

Player	FG-FGA	FT-FTA	Reb.	Ass.	Pts.
K. Malone	7–20	8–14	7	5	22
Edwards	14–19	1–2	7	3	30
Eaton	2–4	0–0	10	0	4
J. Malone	11–20	4–4	3	3	26
Stockton	8–12	2–2	2	19	20
Brown	1–3	0–0	1	0	2
Rudd	1–2	0–0	2	3	2
Austin	1–2	0–0	1	0	2
Corbin	1–3	0–0	3	0	2
Benoit	1–2	0–0	3	0	2
TOTAL	47–87	15–22	39	33	112

3-Point Goals: 3–5 (Stockton 2–3, Edwards 1–1, Rudd 0–1)

CLEVELAND

Player	FG-FGA	FT-FTA	Reb.	Ass.	Pts.
Nance	4–10	4–4	9	3	12
Bennett	1–1	2–2	2	0	4
Daugherty	8–15	3–4	12	4	19
Ehlo	5–12	2–4	6	4	14
Price	4–13	7–7	1	7	17
Williams	1–4	4–6	9	1	6
James	7–11	1–2	0	0	19
Brandon	5–9	0–0	2	5	10
Battle	4–10	4–4	2	2	12
TOTAL	39–85	27–33	43	26	113

3-Point Goals: 8–13 (James 4–5, Price 2–3, Ehlo 2–4, Brandon 0–1)

Attendance: 16,161

CAVALIERS 106, BOSTON CELTICS 87
MAY 14, 1976

Cavalier Fever

It was hard to imagine a time when the Cavaliers had been the most embarrassing team in professional sports, a time when only a few thousand modest souls would actually pay money to watch them play. Locked in what was becoming a titanic duel for the 1976 Eastern Conference championship with the heralded Boston Celtics, the Cavs were sweeping away their losing reputation with each sweet spring night before cacophonous Coliseum crowds. They'd played Boston tough before falling at Boston Garden in Games One and Two, then held off the Celtics in a defensive slugfest to narrow the margin to two games to one. The stage was set for another showdown in Game Four on a Friday night in Richfield.

From the opening moments, Boston found itself behind the eight ball. Legendary forward John Havlicek was forced to leave the game with an injured foot six minutes in, much to the delight of the fired-up sellout crowd. Apparently frustrated at suddenly struggling against a team it had once dominated, the Celtics' seams showed early. Coach Tom Heinsohn was ejected in the second quarter after nearly coming to blows with Cleveland guard Jim Cleamons. As Heinsohn made his way off the court, fans showered him with beer and someone nailed him with a raw egg. "Beautiful Cleveland," Heinsohn groused later. "Twenty-one thousand kids. Crazy."

Still, the Celtics hung tough and took a two-point halftime lead. Tied ten times through the first three quarters, the teams traded punches into the fourth, when the Cavs finally pulled away. Clinging to a one-point lead with 8:35 remaining, the Cavs embarked on a 16–2 run sparked by Austin Carr, who scored thirteen points in the final period. Behind the radar shooting of Bingo Smith, who hit thirteen of seventeen shots, Cleveland shot a robust 56 percent from the floor and topped 100 points for the first time in the postseason. The wired crowd gave the beloved Cavaliers twenty standing ovations—one more than they'd earned in the thrilling Game Seven conference semifinal victory over Washington two weeks earlier.

While Smith and Carr were certainly catalysts, the real hero was veteran Nate Thurmond. Thrust into the starting center role when Jim Chones went down with a broken foot in the final practice before the Boston series, the thirty-seven-year old Thurmond doubled his playing time and motivated the Cavs with his inspired, energetic play. "We're playing right into his hands," Boston's Paul Silas confessed afterward. "We're trying to force things inside and power is his game."

"Nate was magnificent," Jim Brewer said. "Nate played such a great game," Carr added, "he demoralized them." The ageless wonder from Akron scored twelve points, ripped down eight rebounds, and racked up six blocked shots. Dan Coughlin noted Thurmond had "the wingspan of a 747 and the spirit of '76." With Thurmond clogging up the middle and dominating future Hall of Fame center Dave Cowens, the Celtics were held to a harmless thirty-six points in the second half.

When the final buzzer sounded, the Cavs had hung a nineteen-point defeat on the Celtics—their worst defeat of the playoffs—and tied the best-of-seven series at two games apiece. "We beat 'em pretty convincingly tonight, didn't we?" Thurmond said sheepishly. Despite playing without their leading scorer, the Cavs had turned what was once thought to be nothing more than a coronation ceremony for the Celtics into a dogfight. The franchise's first playoff run was well on its way to becoming the stuff of legend, as, for the first time, the city of Cleveland was head over heels in love with its basketball team.

Plain Dealer sports editor Hal Lebovitz put it best the morning after the Celtic thumping: "The Cavalier Fever has burst through the thermometer." Yet no one in Cleveland wanted a cure.

Arriving as a virtual unknown in a controversial trade in 1988, forward Larry Nance became one of the most pivotal players in Cleveland history—reflected by a dominating shot-blocking exhibition against New York in 1989 and a magnificent playoff performance in Boston Garden in 1992. Robin Witek/*Akron Beacon Journal.*

Showing resolve not present when the expansion Cavaliers lost to Philadelphia by 54 points a month earlier, Cleveland center Luther Rackley (left) defends a shot attempt by 76ers guard Archie Clark. Rackley was one of seven Cavs to score in double figures as Cleveland avenged a humiliating loss with a 114–101 triumph over Philly on December 27, 1970. Cleveland State University's *Cleveland Press* Collection.

As much a part of the fabric of Cavalier history as any player or coach, broadcaster Joe Tait has relayed the play-by-play action of thousands of Cavs games. His honesty and straight talk during the dark days of Ted Stepien's disastrous tenure as Cavs owner led to Tait's dismissal in 1981—and consequently, one of the most passionate displays of fan appreciation in Cleveland sports history. *Akron Beacon Journal.*

Below: With his trademark long blonde hair and gritty, intense play, guard Craig Ehlo (right) was one of the greatest clutch players in Cavalier history, symbolized by a Christmas miracle he delivered against Utah on December 23, 1991. Susan Kirkman/*Akron Beacon Journal.*

When Cleveland's leading scorer Jim Chones broke his foot just before the 1976 Eastern Conference finals against Boston, it was up to ageless backup center Nate Thurmond (right) to handle Celtics' star center Dave Cowens (left). In the fourth game of a ferocious series, Thurmond scored twelve points, ripped down eight rebounds, and blocked six shots to help the Cavs tie the series at two games apiece. Cleveland State University's *Cleveland Press* Collection.

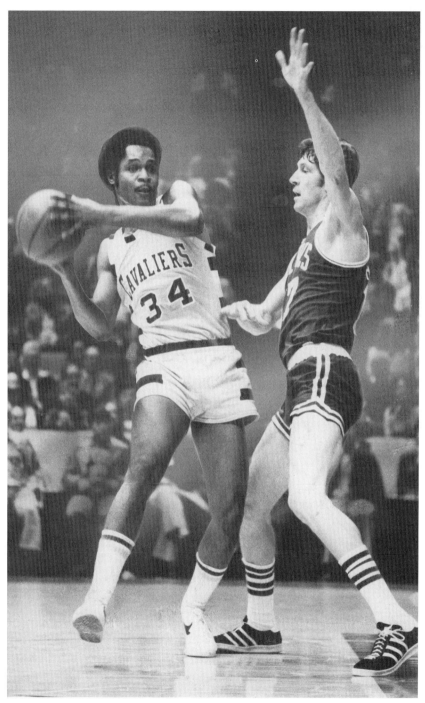

With a magical season teetering on the edge of collapse, Austin Carr (left) exploded for seventeen points in just twenty-five minutes of action off the bench to spark the Cavaliers to a gritty 83–78 win over Boston in Game Three of the 1976 Eastern Conference finals. Cleveland State University's *Cleveland Press* Collection.

A moment that will forever live in Cleveland sports infamy: with Craig Ehlo in his face, Chicago guard Michael Jordan hangs in the air just long enough to get off a nearly impossible shot at the buzzer of the deciding game of a first-round playoff series on May 7, 1989. "The Shot," as it came to be known, gave the Bulls a one-point win, ended the Cavaliers' storybook season, and served as the fork in the road for both franchises for the decade to come. Ott Gangle/*Akron Beacon Journal.*

Austin Carr (left) holds the ball aloft triumphantly and Hall of Fame guard Jerry West (center) wears an expression of disbelief as the buzzer sounds to conclude the Cavaliers' stunning 124–120 victory over the mighty Los Angeles Lakers on March 22, 1972. Four days later, the Lakers would set an NBA record for victories in a season with sixty-nine. Cleveland State University's *Cleveland Press* Collection.

LeBron James performs his pregame ritual of tossing talcum powder into the air while dramatically spreading his arms prior to a playoff game against the Detroit Pistons. James, coming off perhaps the greatest individual performance in NBA playoff history in Game Five of the 2007 Eastern Conference finals against Detroit, would see his draft day promise fulfilled two nights later, when Cleveland was indeed lit up like Las Vegas. Phil Masturzo/*Akron Beacon Journal.*

Right: With all eyes focused on LeBron James, rookie guard Daniel "Boobie" Gibson (left) became the unlikely hero of Game Six of the Eastern Conference finals against Detroit on June 2, 2007. Gibson drained five three-pointers to rally the Cavs past the Pistons and secure the franchise's first trip to the NBA Finals. Ed Suba Jr./*Akron Beacon Journal.*

The greatest moment in Cleveland Cavaliers history—guard Dick Snyder launches an arching shot over the outstretched arms of Washington's Phil Chenier with four seconds left in Game Seven of the 1976 Eastern Conference semifinals. Snyder's shot was the grand finale of a two-week drama that became known as the "Miracle of Richfield." Paul Tepley.

	1	2	3	4	
Celtics	23	28	19	17	=87
Cavaliers	27	22	24	33	=106

BOSTON

Player	FG-FGA	FT-FTA	Reb.	Ass.	Pts.
Silas	2–3	2–2	9	2	6
Havlicek	0–0	0–0	0	0	0
Cowens	5–20	3–4	18	4	13
Scott	7–16	5–6	2	2	19
White	10–26	3–3	8	2	23
McDonald	0–7	0–0	0	0	0
Stacom	2–6	0–0	1	1	4
Kuberski	2–4	2–2	2	3	6
Nelson	3–7	10–10	5	1	16
Ard	0–0	0–0	1	1	0
Anderson	0–1	0–0	0	0	0
TOTAL	31–90	25–27	46	16	87

CLEVELAND

Player	FG-FGA	FT-FTA	Reb.	Ass.	Pts.
Smith	13–17	1–1	2	3	27
Brewer	3–6	0–1	11	5	6
Thurmond	6–10	0–2	8	3	12
Cleamons	7–12	2–3	5	8	16
Snyder	4–9	0–0	4	1	8
Witte	2–4	2–2	2	2	6
Russell	6–11	0–0	3	1	12
Carr	7–15	2–4	3	2	16
Walker	0–2	1–2	1	1	1
Lambert	1–1	0–0	3	0	2
Garrett	0–0	0–0	0	0	0
TOTAL	49–87	8–15	42	26	106

Attendance: 21,564

CAVALIERS 97, LOS ANGELES LAKERS 95
DECEMBER 5, 1987

Some Magic of Their Own

It was as if the Los Angeles Lakers were playing a younger version of themselves, the team they had been before going on a legendary tear through the 1980s by winning five NBA titles in nine years and redefining "cool" in professional sports. From the trademark slicked-back hair of coach Pat Riley to the smorgasbord of celebrities who'd attend Laker home games at the Great Western Forum to the "Showtime" quality of their dynamic fast breaks, the Lakers transcended the medium of sports and had become a pop culture phenomenon. But before all that, the Lakers of the late 1970s were a competitive team that was just starting to learn how to win.

When the defending-champion Lakers arrived in Richfield on a cold December night in 1987, they met a competitive, young Cavaliers team on the brink of entering the upper echelon of the league—much like the Lakers of a decade earlier.

Cleveland, which hadn't posted a winning record in ten years, got off to a slow start again in '87, dropping eight of its first twelve, while the Lakers charged out to their best start ever, ripping off eight straight victories to start the year. Though the Cavs had lost seven straight home games to Los Angeles, a sellout crowd of better than 20,000 fans filed through the turnstiles to see if the hometown team could hold its own against the league's best.

From the opening moments, it was clear the defending champs would have their hands full. Hitting 61 percent of their first-half shots, the Cavs raced to an eight-point halftime lead and took a five-point advantage into the final period. And Cleveland was beating the fast-paced Lakers at their own game, outscoring the Showtime boys 20–2 in fast break points while blocking ten shots—including a monster stuff by the Cavs' six-foot-six forward Tyrone

Corbin of a dunk attempt by the legendary Kareem Abdul-Jabbar, who stood eight inches taller. With the crowd roaring and the teams matching each other move for move down the stretch, this early-season game took on a decidedly playoff flavor—not that many of the Cavs had any idea what that felt like.

The Lakers rallied from a six-point deficit with just over two minutes to play and had a chance to take charge when guard Magic Johnson was sent to the free-throw line for two shots with fifteen seconds remaining and the score tied. Johnson missed both and the Cavs were granted an opportunity to win the game with their final possession. With the clock running down under five seconds, Mark Price tossed a pass to an open Brad Daugherty on the wing, and Daugherty fired a fifteen-foot jumper. The ball rattled off the rim and fell away, but with a second left, Corbin—who'd barely made the team as an undrafted free agent two years earlier—came crashing through the right side and tipped it back up with his right hand. "Crash the boards," Corbin said later. "Crash the boards—that's all I had on my mind."

As the buzzer sounded, the basketball danced around the rim, then finally gently fell through the net, giving the Cavs one of the most exciting and satisfying victories in franchise history. "How big was this?" Price asked reporters in the locker room, then answered his own question with a simple yet dramatic statement: "We beat the Lakers."

Perhaps more significantly, Bill Livingston wrote the Cavs had "sounded a note for that portion of the professional basketball world that does not perform before the Laker Girls, is not expected to believe in Magic, and is not the apple of Jack Nicholson's sun-glassed eyes."

Though the Cavaliers would only hover around the .500 mark for the remainder of the 1987–88 season, the Los Angeles win served as an announcement that the Cavs were no longer a perennial fifty-loss team. Four months later, Cleveland would secure its first playoff berth in three years. And when the Cavs began a majestic run through the regular season a year later, Magic Johnson would pass the torch his Lakers had carried for a decade, labeling the Cavaliers as "the team of the '90s."

	1	2	3	4	
Lakers	22	27	25	21	=95
Cavaliers	22	35	22	18	=97

LOS ANGELES

Player	FG-FGA	FT-FTA	Reb.	Ass.	Pts.
Rambis	3–4	2–3	3	1	8
Green	3–9	5–8	9	1	11
Abdul-Jabbar	7–16	7–8	5	2	21
Scott	9–19	0–0	5	1	19
Johnson	6–16	7–8	9	9	19
Cooper	2–10	0–0	5	6	5
Thompson	4–10	2–2	7	0	10
Wagner	1–1	0–0	0	2	2
TOTAL	35–85	23–29	43	22	95

3-Point Goals: 2–7 (Cooper 1–3, Scott 1–4)

CLEVELAND

Player	FG-FGA	FT-FTA	Reb.	Ass.	Pts.
Hubbard	7–11	5–6	4	0	19
Williams	0–1	0–0	6	3	0
Daugherty	4–11	6–6	9	4	14
Ehlo	4–8	0–0	1	3	8
Price	5–8	0–0	0	8	10
Johnson	4–7	0–0	1	5	8
Corbin	7–11	2–4	7	1	16
Curry	7–15	0–0	2	4	14
West	4–8	0–2	8	1	8
TOTAL	42–80	13–18	38	29	97

3-Point Goals: 0–2 (Curry 0–2)

Attendance: 20,015

CAVALIERS 100, NEW YORK KNICKS 95
APRIL 3, 1975

Walking on the Moon

"If I said four years ago," Bill Fitch said, "that we would be playing for a playoff spot now with the Knicks in front of 20,000 people, they would say, 'Yeah, and I'll walk on the moon.'"

And yet, it had happened. In the second-to-last game of their fifth season, the Cavaliers—who had averaged a whopping fifty-seven losses per year over their first four—would host the legendary New York Knicks with the fifth and final Eastern Conference playoff spot hanging in the balance. Not only was a big crowd expected, but the game would be broadcast over the Armed Forces Radio Network, marking the first time a Cavs game had ever been carried on a global basis. It was a scenario Cavs' owner Nick Mileti, who had grown up admiring the Knicks, only dreamed of when he founded the team.

A Cavs' loss would clinch a playoff bid for New York, while a victory would keep their postseason hopes alive for two more days until the season finale against the Kansas City-Omaha Kings. An unusual April winter storm, exacerbated by dangerously high winds, blasted Cleveland that day, snarling traffic and waylaying many citizens in their homes. Yet ninety minutes before tip-off that night, fans were lined up outside the Coliseum gates waiting to get in. By 6:30, the parking lot was jammed, and for an hour before the tip, fans screamed themselves hoarse. "Now I know how other teams feel when they come to Madison Square Garden," Knicks' star Walt Frazier said. Once the scourge of the league, the Cavs had drawn 20,239 fans to their home finale—at the time the largest crowd in NBA history. And the fans would get their money's worth in a back-and-forth contest that would see twelve ties and countless momentum swings.

The Cavs came out sharp and soared to an early six-point lead, but the Knicks caught fire in the second quarter and took a four-point advantage to the locker room. Cleveland rallied and carried a two-point margin into the biggest fourth quarter in franchise history. The Cavs appeared poised to coast to victory when they streaked to a 92–82 lead with 6:25 left, but the veteran Knicks responded with a 13–4 run to cut the deficit to a single point with 1:19 remaining. Things looked even worse when New York regained possession, but Cleveland's Jim Cleamons came up with a huge steal, then was fouled and nailed two free throws to snap a four-minute scoring drought for the home team.

The inexperienced Cavaliers showed they still had some growing up to do moments later when forward Jim Brewer was called for traveling on a fast break after ripping down a rebound with the Cavs still up three with thirty seconds left. But with the game on the line, the Cleveland defense rose to the occasion. First, guard Dick Snyder blocked a Frazier shot with twenty seconds left, then Cleamons swatted an Earl Monroe attempt with six ticks showing. Jim Chones collected the loose ball and fired it downcourt to Brewer, who slammed it home to seal the victory to the delight of the berserk home crowd. "If our fans yell that loud Sunday," Fitch said afterward, "we'll hear them in Omaha."

It was a game of multiple Cleveland heroes. Snyder, who hadn't scored a point in the Cavs' previous game, exploded for twenty-two on eleven-of-sixteen shooting. Cleamons rebounded from a miserable start, missing six of his first seven shots, to score seventeen points in the second half, eleven in the critical fourth quarter. Cleamons and Snyder matched the heralded Frazier and Monroe point for point, assist for assist, and steal for steal, and even gathered ten rebounds to the New York duo's nine. "Cleveland has always played us tough," Frazier admitted afterward. "They kept their poise. They made the baskets they had to make."

In the first clutch game in team history, the Cavaliers responded, truly looking like a playoff team. And for fans who had suffered through the first four miserable seasons, it was indeed like watching them walk on the moon.

	1	2	3	4	
Knicks	22	31	20	22	=95
Cavaliers	28	21	26	25	=100

NEW YORK

Player	FG-FGA	FT-FTA	Reb.	Ass.	Pts.
Bradley	2–10	0–0	1	3	4
Jackson	5–12	1–2	13	2	11
Gianelli	7–14	2–3	9	5	16
Frazier	8–17	4–5	7	6	20
Monroe	8–17	5–6	2	3	21
Wingo	3–4	3–3	4	0	9
Barnett	6–7	2–2	1	0	14
Bell	0–0	0–0	0	0	0
TOTAL	39–81	17–21	37	19	95

CLEVELAND

Player	FG-FGA	FT-FTA	Reb.	Ass.	Pts.
Smith	6–15	6–6	1	8	18
Brewer	7–11	0–2	13	2	14
Chones	8–13	0–0	7	2	16
Snyder	11–16	0–0	6	3	22
Cleamons	8–16	3–4	4	6	19
Foster	0–3	0–0	0	0	0
Davis	2–4	2–2	1	0	6
Patterson	0–0	0–0	2	0	0
Carr	2–4	1–2	2	1	5
TOTAL	44–82	12–16	36	22	100

Attendance: 20,239

CAVALIERS 99, CHICAGO BULLS 85
MAY 25, 1992

Maalox Moment

For five years, Mark Price had been the heart and soul of the Cleveland Cavaliers.

He'd gone from an afterthought draft day acquisition to the team's catalyst. Once Price became the starting point guard, the Cavs reached the playoffs three straight seasons. When he tore knee ligaments a month into the 1990–91 campaign, the team fell apart, losing forty-nine games. And then when he returned earlier than expected the following November, the Cavs started one of the greatest turnarounds in NBA history, embarking on a franchise-best fifty-seven-win season and notching two playoff series victories for the first time.

And now, with the biggest game of the year looming before him, the team's heart and soul couldn't keep down a peanut butter sandwich.

After the Cavs were humbled by Chicago on a Saturday afternoon in Game Three of the 1992 Eastern Conference finals, Price started feeling queasy. After not being able to keep anything down and missing practice the next day, Price spent Sunday night hooked up to an IV at the Cleveland Clinic. When he arrived at Richfield Coliseum for Game Four on Memorial Day afternoon, he was pale and weak, not having eaten for two days. It was not the time to be facing the defending world champions with the possibility of falling down three games to one in a best-of-seven playoff series. Appropriately, a Cleveland fan posted a makeshift cardboard sign alongside Interstate 77 reading "Maalox Moment Next Right."

Price, downing antacid throughout, stayed on the floor and contributed as much as he could, though he had to leave the game midway through the third quarter and return to the locker room to avoid demonstrating his digestive difficulties to a sellout crowd and a nationwide television audience. It was actually the second straight game Price had been nullified. The Bulls had matched the six-foot-six Michael Jordan with Price to start Game Three, and the Cavs' offense was thrown into reverse as the Bulls sprinted to an insurmountable 26–4 lead. Now, with Price stymied by his own malfunctioning innards, the Cavs had to dig deep to survive.

And, with a strategic wrinkle of their own, they did. Lenny Wilkens shifted the Cavs' base offense and brought Brad Daugherty from his usual spot underneath up to the top of the key, where he essentially directed the offense. The Bulls had trouble adapting and fell behind by fifteen points in a second quarter that included a few tense moments. When Jordan and Cavs' reserve forward Danny Ferry got tangled up in a mass of humanity on an inbound play, Ferry flung his arms out to break free and struck Jordan in the face. The Bulls' star cocked his fist to deliver a retaliatory blow but other players intervened. Ferry was called for a technical foul and ejected from the game, which now took on an even fiercer tone with more emphasis on defense.

Later, Jordan and Craig Ehlo cracked heads while chasing after a loose ball, and both remained on the floor for several minutes. The teams would combine for just thirty-three points in the third quarter, while All-Star Chicago forward Scottie Pippen was held scoreless in the second and only managed thirteen points for the game. Jordan—the biggest Cavs killer of them all—was "held" to thirty-five points, though he had to take thirty-three shots to get them.

The Cavs maintained control through the third quarter despite Price's absence. Then, two minutes into the fourth quarter, the Coliseum crowd erupted as Price came jogging out of the tunnel to rejoin the team on the bench. Soon after, he reentered the game. "I felt I needed to be out there from a leadership standpoint," Price said. "I wasn't looking to score. I just tried to get the ball in people's hands." The Cavs' catalyst still wound up with thirteen points, two assists, and a rebound for the day.

But when a fourteen-point second-half lead was trimmed to four with under four minutes to play and a Cleveland possession about to implode with the shot clock winding down, the Cavs needed *someone* to score. As the shot clock reached one, journeyman forward Mike Sanders launched a desperation three-pointer from the left wing. The ball stroked through the hoop at the buzzer. The lead was back to seven and the Bulls' momentum had vanished. It was only the second three-point shot Sanders had made all season, but it came at the absolutely perfect moment. "If we don't get that shot," Ehlo said later, "our throats are cut."

The Cavs coasted to a fourteen-point victory, the exclamation-point bucket coming on a layup following a drive by the weary Price. Thanks to a courageous performance by their leader and resourceful team play, the Cavs had tied the series on little more than intestinal fortitude.

	1	2	3	4	
Bulls	24	19	17	25	=85
Cavaliers	30	25	16	28	=99

CHICAGO

Player	FG-FGA	FT-FTA	Reb.	Ass.	Pts.
Grant	2–7	3–4	15	3	7
Pippen	5–11	2–3	10	4	13
Cartwright	2–4	0–2	2	1	4
Jordan	15–33	4–5	5	6	35
Paxson	5–7	0–1	0	3	11
Williams	1–5	0–0	5	0	2
Armstrong	2–7	0–0	0	1	4
Perdue	0–1	0–0	0	0	0
King	0–1	0–0	1	0	0
Hodges	0–4	1–2	1	0	1
Levingston	4–7	0–0	2	0	8
TOTAL	36–87	10–17	41	18	85

3-Point Goals: 3–8 (Pippen 1–1, Paxson 1–1, Jordan 1–3, Hodges 0–3)

CLEVELAND

Player	FG-FGA	FT-FTA	Reb.	Ass.	Pts.
Nance	8–17	6–8	11	4	22
Sanders	3–4	2–2	2	3	9
Daugherty	2–7	10–13	14	6	14
Ehlo	7–16	3–3	2	1	21
Price	4–8	4–4	1	2	13
Brandon	1–6	0–0	3	5	2
Williams	7–9	4–6	3	4	18
Ferry	0–0	0–0	2	0	0
TOTAL	32–67	29–36	38	25	99

3-Point Goals: 6–10 (Ehlo 4–7, Sanders 1–1, Price 1–2)

Attendance: 20,273

CAVALIERS 121, WASHINGTON WIZARDS 120 (OT)
MAY 3, 2006

Rite of Passage

In many ways, it wasn't so much that the Cleveland Cavaliers had made the playoffs for the first time in eight years but that LeBron James had made it for the first time. NBA Commissioner David Stern called James's entry into the 2006 postseason a "rite of passage," inferring that now The Chosen One could prove he was as good as the hype surrounding him, just as Magic Johnson, Larry Bird, and Michael Jordan had done before.

Yet the Cavs, winners of fifty games in the regular season, faced a serious challenge in the first round with a best-of-seven series against the dangerous Washington Wizards. After splitting the first two games in Cleveland, James hit the game-winning shot in the waning moments of Game Three for a two-games-to-one Cavs' lead. But the Wizards responded with a critical win in Game Four to send the series back to Quicken Loans Arena for the pivotal fifth game.

Though James was averaging thirty-four points per game in the series, the Cavs knew other players would have to step up. Likewise, the Cleveland defense had to figure out a way to slow down Washington guard Gilbert Arenas, who was matching James highlight for highlight. And in Game Five, James and Arenas would put on a dazzling show of one-upmanship. The teams battled all night, neither able to pull away. James and Arenas continued their scoring display, but the Cavaliers hit a snag in the third quarter when their point machine was forced to the bench with foul trouble. In his absence, guards Ronald "Flip" Murray and Larry Hughes stepped up. Murray scored ten of his twelve points in the third, while Hughes shook off a postseason scoring slump and hit for nine of his twenty-four points in the quarter. Hughes, who had played in Washington the previous three years, had only been averaging ten points per game in the playoffs, five off his regular season average.

Yet for all the heroics, neither team could secure victory in regulation. The Cavs held a seven-point lead with just over a minute left, but the Wizards rallied to tie. After James missed a fadeaway jumper at the buzzer, the teams barreled into overtime, where the Cavs sprinted to a four-point lead a minute in, thanks to a six-point surge from reserve guard and Canton native Eric Snow. Washington trimmed the lead to one with under a minute left, and then Arenas stripped the basketball from Hughes and drove in for the go-ahead layup with 30.5 seconds remaining.

After Cleveland retook the lead, Arenas answered again with a pair of free throws with 3.6 seconds showing to put Washington up 120–119, giving Arenas forty-four points on the night to James's forty-three. It was James's turn to answer. He took an inbound pass from Hughes but resisted the urge to put up a quick shot. "I didn't just want to catch it and fire up a jumper," James said. "I saw Antwan Jamison closing out hard, so I just tight-roped the baseline." With three defenders closing on him, James slipped between Michael Ruffin, Brendan Haywood, and Arenas and laid the ball into the basket with 0.9 showing on the clock as the sellout Q crowd exploded. James had now outscored Arenas, forty-five to forty-four, and when the Wizards were unable to hit a desperation shot at the buzzer, the Cavs had a three-games-to-two edge in the series. James marched through the mob scene, which had flooded the floor, with arms raised triumphantly in what would become an iconic image in team history.

For the second time in a week, LeBron James had won a playoff game with a last-second basket, leading him further along his much-anticipated rite of passage.

	1	2	3	4	OT	
Wizards	27	24	30	26	13	=120
Cavaliers	25	27	33	22	14	=121

WASHIINGTON

Player	FG-FGA	FT-FTA	Reb.	Ass.	Pts.
Butler	8–16	4–6	11	5	20
Jamison	13–24	3–6	5	2	32
Haywood	0–1	1–2	2	0	1
Arenas	14–24	10–10	5	4	44
Jeffries	4–7	0–0	4	2	8
E. Thomas	0–1	2–2	2	0	2
Daniels	5–11	3–3	2	7	13
Ruffin	0–0	0–0	3	3	0
B. Thomas	0–0	0–0	0	0	0
TOTAL	44–84	23–29	34	23	120

3-Point Goals: 9–20 (Arenas 6–9, Jamison 3–7, Jeffries 0–1, Daniels 0–3)

CLEVELAND

Player	FG-FGA	FT-FTA	Reb.	Ass.	Pts.
James	14–23	17–18	7	6	45
Gooden	3–7	0–0	11	0	6
Ilgauskas	3–6	0–2	5	0	6
Snow	8–12	2–3	3	3	18
Hughes	8–19	7–10	3	3	24
Marshall	2–3	2–2	6	0	6
Murray	5–9	2–2	4	2	12
Varejao	1–2	2–6	7	1	4
Jones	0–0	0–0	0	0	0
TOTAL	44–81	32–43	46	15	121

3-Point Goals: 1–5 (Hughes 1–3, James 0–1, Murray 0–1)

Attendance: 20,562

#25

CAVALIERS 111, NEW YORK KNICKS 109
FEBRUARY 20, 1972

The Miracle of Euclid Avenue

The Cavs hadn't won many games over their first two seasons, losing 114 of their first 147, but here and there they'd managed to pick up their share of token "legitimate" victories. In fact, by February 1972, Cleveland had defeated every team in the Eastern Conference but one. And while the team and its beleaguered fans would love nothing more than to put the final checkmark on the list, a victory over the New York Knicks seemed highly unlikely.

On their way back to the playoffs, the Knicks arrived at Cleveland Arena with a strong 40–23 mark, having defeated the Cavaliers by fifteen points eight days before and by twenty in mid-December. And even with New York forward Bill Bradley sidelined with an injured calf, the game followed the same blueprint in the early going as the visitors roared to a twenty-one-point first-quarter lead. The second-largest Arena crowd of the season sat glumly silent, convinced the Cavs were on their way to yet another defeat. "We took off like gangbusters," New York forward Jerry Lucas said. "It was too easy and we probably relaxed and the momentum changed."

Ever so slowly, the Cavs chipped away at New York's apparently insurmountable advantage. It was down to twelve at the half, then Cleveland caught fire in the third quarter, narrowing the margin to a single point at 71–70 with 4:01 left in the period. But Lucas drilled three straight shots to put the Knicks out comfortably once again, and they took a six-point lead into the fourth.

Time and again, it appeared the more experienced Knicks had finally delivered the knockout blow, only to watch the Cavs keep swinging. Cleveland guard Charlie Davis came off the bench to hit two long jumpers to tie the game at ninety-two. The Knicks then scored five straight, but the Cavs rallied to tie it again at 101. After a Lucas free throw and a Dave DeBusschere tip-in, New

York led by three, but Cleveland responded with its most impressive run of the game. The Cavaliers delighted the suddenly electric home crowd with a 10–1 run, highlighted by an eight-foot jumper by guard Butch Beard, which gave the Cavs a 107–105 lead with fifty-eight seconds remaining. Beard, who had been slumping in recent weeks, exploded for twenty-one points on the night, topped only by rookie Austin Carr's twenty-five. Veteran center Walt Wesley also rose to the occasion, ripping down thirteen rebounds to go along with his eighteen points.

Cleveland stretched the lead to 111–105 before the Knicks hit the final two baskets of the game to make the final spread two points. The Cavs, a team that averaged just 105 points per game for the year, scored ninety-eight in the final three periods alone to atone for a miserable start to secure the biggest victory in the young history of the franchise. In so doing, they completed their victory dance card in the Eastern Conference, knocking off a team that would win twenty-five more games than themselves and then go on to capture the conference title.

Perhaps more impressive than simply beating the Knicks was rallying to victory from twenty-one points down—something the Cavaliers hadn't yet shown they were capable of. "Imagine Luxembourg defeating Russia in a war or Phyllis Diller stealing Richard Burton away from Liz," Bill Nichols wrote. "What the Cavs did was even more improbable.

"The Cavaliers last night pulled off the Miracle of Euclid Avenue."

	1	2	3	4	
Knicks	32	24	30	23	=109
Cavaliers	13	31	36	31	=111

NEW YORK

Player	FG	FT-FTA	Pts.
Barnett	4	5–7	13
DeBusschere	11	6–6	28
Frazier	7	5–7	19
Jackson	2	3–6	7
Lucas	10	3–5	23
Mast	0	0–0	0
Meminger	1	0–0	2
Monroe	6	3–5	15
Paulk	0	0–0	0
Rackley	1	0–1	2
TOTAL	42	25–37	109

CLEVELAND

Player	FG	FT-FTA	Pts.
Beard	8	5–8	21
Carr	11	3–3	25
Davis	4	5–5	13
Howard	2	0–0	4
Johnson	0	0–0	0
Patterson	5	0–2	10
Roberson	4	1–1	9
Smith	3	5–5	11
Warren	0	0–0	0
Wesley	9	0–0	18
TOTAL	46	19–24	111

Attendance: 8,877

CAVALIERS 148, MIAMI HEAT 80
DECEMBER 17, 1991

Don't Make the Cavaliers Mad

Putting it frankly, the Cleveland Cavaliers were pissed off.

A season that suddenly garnered lofty expectations with the early return of Mark Price, who had been absent a year due to a knee injury, had taken a sudden dip. A string of eight wins in nine games coinciding with Price's return was followed by a mediocre seven-game string in which the Cavs lost three, including inexcusable two-point losses to subpar squads Dallas and Miami.

Thus Cleveland came into a Tuesday night rematch with the Heat at Richfield Coliseum with a modest 12–8 record, still stinging from their lethargic performance in Miami the Wednesday before. They felt they had to prove themselves as a legitimate playoff team, both to their fans and the rest of the conference. On what turned out to be a historic night, the Cavs were successful on both fronts.

Just over 10,000 fans braved the cold temperatures and trekked the snowy roads to Richfield, where they saw the Cavs start hot and never cool off. With every facet of their offense clicking, the Cavaliers scored seventy-three points in the first half and roared to a twenty-point lead. But things didn't really get interesting until the second half, when the Cavs put on a show unequalled in the history of the NBA.

With the five starters spending much of the final two quarters on the bench, Cleveland actually extended its lead. With the reserves playing just as well, the Cavs scored thirty-three more points in the third and led 105–67 going into the fourth, when things got really ridiculous. Cleveland exploded for forty-two points in the final twelve minutes, while holding the Heat to thirteen. Miami was held to a franchise-low twenty-seven points in the second half—fewer points than Cleveland scored in any quarter, while the Cavs shot better than

57 percent from the floor and 83 percent from the free-throw line. They out-rebounded Miami 59–41 and dished out twenty-nine assists. Every Cleveland player scored at least five points, and eight hit double figures. At one point in the second half, the Cavs embarked on a 75–20 run. All this against a team they'd lost to six days before. *"Well, one thing's for sure,"* Joe Tait told his radio audience at the game's conclusion. *"Don't make the Cavaliers mad."*

"Everything was going in," said reserve guard Steve Kerr. "We didn't want to pour it on, but when you're one of the last guys on the bench, you're not going to hold back."

When the buzzer sounded, the Cavs had etched their place in basketball history. The final score was 148–80, and the whopping margin of sixty-eight points broke the NBA record for largest margin of victory which had stood for nineteen years after a 162–99 win by the Lakers over Golden State in 1972. It was a twenty-five-point improvement over the franchise's previous biggest win and also marked the most points the Cavs had ever scored in a regulation game. "That was incredible," Lenny Wilkens said. "It was a great display of basketball. They shot the ball, they rebounded, and they passed. It doesn't happen like this very often, but every once in a while it comes together like this."

"We played awful in Miami," Brad Daugherty said. "We wanted to come back and it just snowballed. I couldn't believe it when I looked up and we were ahead by sixty points. It was a lot of fun."

And they'd done it against a team that would wind up qualifying for the playoffs four months later. More importantly for the Cavs, the record-setting victory fueled an eleven-game winning streak that propelled them to a fifty-seven-win season and a jaunt to the Eastern Conference finals.

	1	2	3	4	
Heat	24	29	14	13	=80
Cavaliers	34	39	33	42	=148

MIAMI

Player	FG-FGA	FT-FTA	Reb.	Ass.	Pts.
Long	3–8	1–1	3	0	7
Burton	3–8	1–1	0	3	7
Seikaly	4–7	1–1	7	0	9
Rice	3–8	0–0	5	3	9
Smith	7–13	0–2	1	3	15
Edwards	4–10	2–2	2	1	10
Kessler	2–5	1–2	5	3	5
Coles	0–8	0–0	7	3	0
Askins	2–11	0–0	5	0	5
Ogg	2–5	0–0	1	0	4
Babic	1–4	0–0	5	2	2
Morton	2–6	2–2	0	0	7
TOTAL	33–93	8–11	41	18	80

3-Point Goals: 6–14 (Rice 3–3, Morton 1–2, Smith 1–3, Askins 1–5, Coles 0–1)

CLEVELAND

Player	FG-FGA	FT-FTA	Reb.	Ass.	Pts.
Nance	4–8	1–2	4	3	9
Bennett	4–11	3–4	10	2	11
Daugherty	6–11	5–7	7	3	17
Ehlo	3–5	0–0	4	3	7
Price	8–10	0–0	3	11	18
Brandon	4–7	0–0	1	7	8
Williams	5–8	6–6	6	0	16
Battle	7–11	4–4	1	2	18
Oliver	4–6	3–4	2	3	11
Ferry	5–10	0–0	11	1	11
James	7–14	2–2	8	1	17
Kerr	2–2	0–0	2	3	5
TOTAL	59–103	24–29	59	39	148

3-Point Goals: 6–11 (Price 2–2, Ferry 1–1, Kerr 1–1, Ehlo 1–2, James 1–4, Oliver 0–1)

Attendance: 10,487

CAVALIERS 113, CHICAGO BULLS 112
FEBRUARY 17, 1992

Mistake-Free

While the Cavaliers struggled through injury and adversity in the early 1990s, the Chicago Bulls were busy defining themselves as one of the greatest teams in NBA history. Since eliminating Cleveland in a fateful first-round playoff series in 1989, the Bulls had replaced the Detroit Pistons as the Eastern Conference's kingpin and in 1991 captured the first of what would become a string of six world titles.

Along the way, Michael Jordan and the Bulls simply owned the Cavs. His game-winning shot in Game Five of the '89 playoff series clinched the first of thirteen consecutive Chicago victories over Cleveland stretching over nearly three full seasons. And the losses had come in every conceivable fashion: blowouts, buzzer-beating buckets, blown leads, spoiled comebacks. The Bulls simply had the Cavaliers' number. "We've played some good games against them and lost," Brad Daugherty said. "We have to be mistake-free against them."

Even when the Cavs finally put it together in 1991–92 and rejoined the league elite, they still lost two one-sided games to the Bulls and trailed them by eight and a half games in the Central Division going into their third meeting of the season on Presidents' Day evening at Chicago Stadium, where the 42–9 Bulls had won fourteen straight games.

Cleveland came out sharp and played as well as could be expected, shooting 59 percent from the floor and attacking Chicago down low. The Cavs' triple threat of Daugherty, Larry Nance, and Hot Rod Williams helped the Cavs earn a 24–6 free-throw advantage. But as usual, the Bulls rose to the occasion. Celebrating his twenty-ninth birthday, Jordan lit up the Cavs for forty-six points while hitting twenty-one of thirty-two shots. Forward Scottie Pippen scored twenty-four in the first three quarters and helped Chicago take a two-point lead into the fourth.

In what became a wild final period, the Bulls raced to a seven-point lead and appeared on the brink of coasting to a fourteenth consecutive victory over the hard-luck Cavs. But led by their defense, Cleveland clawed back into contention. Sparked by Nance, who held Pippen scoreless in the fourth, the Cavs tied the contest at 103 on a pair of free throws by Williams with 4:03 left. The teams traded punches over the next three minutes. Then the Cavs appeared to sneak into the driver's seat.

Craig Ehlo, who'd endured the unenviable task of guarding Jordan all night, hit a pair of free throws with 44.5 seconds left to put the Cavs up 113–110. But, to no one's surprise, Jordan responded ten seconds later with a twelve-foot fallaway jumper to cut the margin to one. The Cavs tried to melt as much of the remaining time as they could, but an Ehlo pass was intercepted by Chicago forward Horace Grant and the Bulls called time out with six seconds left.

With every soul in the building knowing exactly who the Bulls wanted to get the ball to, the Cavs threw a wrinkle into their defensive strategy. Lenny Wilkens gambled on quickness and put the six-foot-tall Mark Price on Jordan, sacrificing six inches of defense. The gamble worked. Price stuck to Jordan like glue, not allowing him to break open, and Pippen was forced to improvise with a makeshift running fifteen-footer that missed badly just before the buzzer. With that, the Cavs' painful losing streak was over.

"Others have made a bigger deal of this losing streak than we have," Price said afterward. "We knew it was a matter of time before we would beat them."

Thanks to an essentially mistake-free performance, that time had finally come. And after not defeating the Bulls for almost three years, the Cavs' thrilling one-point victory that February night opened the floodgates. Over the next three months, the Cavs would knock off Jordan and Company three more times and go on to actually take the season series from Chicago the following year.

	1	2	3	4	
Cavaliers	25	34	29	25	=113
Bulls	27	33	30	22	=112

CLEVELAND

Player	FG-FGA	FT-FTA	Reb.	Ass.	Pts.
Bennett	2–5	0–0	3	1	4
Nance	6–9	3–4	4	1	15
Daugherty	9–14	7–10	14	4	25
Ehlo	6–9	2–2	7	6	16
Price	9–14	2–2	1	5	23
Williams	6–8	4–5	3	3	16
Brandon	1–4	2–2	1	2	4
Battle	3–7	4–4	0	0	10
Ferry	0–1	0–0	0	0	0
TOTAL	42–71	24–29	33	22	113

3-Point Goals: 5–8 (Price 3–5, Ehlo 2–3)

CHICAGO

Player	FG-FGA	FT-FTA	Reb.	Ass.	Pts.
Pippen	12–21	0–0	9	7	24
Grant	4–8	0–0	11	5	8
Cartwright	2–8	0–2	7	3	4
Paxson	6–7	1–2	0	2	13
Jordan	21–32	4–5	4	6	46
Armstrong	3–6	0–0	0	1	6
Perdue	0–0	0–0	0	1	0
Levingston	0–1	1–2	1	0	1
Hodges	2–6	0–0	1	5	4
King	0–1	0–0	1	0	0
Williams	3–3	0–0	2	0	6
TOTAL	53–93	6–11	36	30	112

3-Point Goals: 0–6 (Pippen 0–1, Paxson 0–1, Jordan 0–1, Hodges 0–3)

Attendance: 18,676

A Night to Be Proud

It was the night every professional sports franchise strives for. Not only was it the first home game of a season loaded with expectations, but the pregame festivities included the hoisting of a championship banner and the presentation of title rings commemorating the epic achievements of the previous season.

This was the setting the struggling Cleveland Cavaliers found waiting for them at the Great Western Forum in Los Angeles on the first Tuesday in November 1985. The Lakers, still glowing from their 1984–85 NBA title and afire once again with a 4–0 start to 1985–86, hadn't missed a beat, while the Cavs had lost the lightning-in-a-bottle magic that had propelled them to the playoffs the previous spring. While the Cavs sloshed to a 1–4 start, the Lakers were simply blowing people away, winning their first four contests by an average of sixteen points while outshooting opponents by double digits and outrebounding them by an average of ten per game.

Making matters worse, the Cavs hadn't won at the Forum in eight years, were winless against dynamic Lakers' coach Pat Riley, and had been handed a twenty-seven-point loss on their last trip to L.A. the previous March. Better than 17,000 would pack into the Forum, marking the Lakers' first-ever sellout for a home opener. All things considered, few outcomes seemed as easy to predict as this one.

The Cavs crept to a seven-point lead in the opening minutes behind the hot shooting of guard World B. Free, but when the Lakers rallied and grabbed a lead late in the first period, they were poised to pull away. Instead, it was the Cavs who took their game to the next level. They turned the tables on the home team to take a seven-point lead into the second period, then hit their next twelve shots and sprinted to a stunning 51–33 lead. In the very building where Magic Johnson, James Worthy, and Company had practically invented the fast break, the Cavaliers were beating the world champs at their own game, scoring fifteen breakaway points in the first eight minutes of the second period. And things would only get better.

After L.A. narrowed the margin to fourteen, Cleveland exploded with a 9–0 run to make it 65–42. Even a sixty-foot-shot by Lakers' forward Michael Cooper at the end of the half couldn't halt the Cavs' momentum. Los Angeles could draw no closer than fourteen points in the second half while the Cleveland lead swelled to as much as twenty-eight. "When it got down to about the six-minute mark, I turned down the bench and said, 'Please, nobody wake me up,'" Cavs' coach George Karl said. "I mean, this was the Lakers, right? That was Magic Johnson, Kareem Abdul-Jabbar, and James Worthy, wasn't it? I just can't believe it."

The disbelief only grew stronger with a glance at the box score. The Cavaliers became the first team that season to outrebound the league's tallest team, 64–53, holding the mighty Kareem to a harmless four boards. Three Cavaliers players scored twenty points or more—Free, point guard John Bagley, and forward Edgar Jones, a career substitute who hit for twenty-four along with twelve rebounds. The upstarts in the pumpkin-orange jerseys had outshot the Lakers 57 to 42 percent and racked up eight blocked shots and nine steals. It was Showtime—Cleveland-style. "I hope we can play better than this," Karl said with a laugh, "but I don't really see how we could."

Add it all together and you come up with the Lakers' worst home loss in 108 games—a convincing defeat that snapped a seventeen-game Forum winning streak and a ten-game Lakers string over Cleveland. More notably, the Cavs had ruined what was supposed to be an emotional night for a franchise and its fans. "It was our biggest night of the year," a somber Riley said afterward. "It was a night to be proud."

Indeed it was—but not for the defending champions.

	1	2	3	4	
Cavaliers	37	38	29	25	=129
Lakers	30	27	28	26	=111

CLEVELAND

Player	FG-FGA	FT-FTA	Reb.	Ass.	Pts.
Hinson	6–8	5–5	8	2	17
Hubbard	4–10	2–4	5	1	10
Turpin	4–6	1–1	2	0	9
Bagley	9–16	2–2	3	11	20
Free	9–14	1–3	2	3	20
Jones	9–14	6–9	12	1	24
Poquette	0–2	0–0	3	0	0
Davis	7–9	3–4	1	2	17
West	3–7	4–6	8	0	10
Minniefield	0–2	0–0	3	7	0
Anderson	0–1	1–2	1	0	1
Whatley	0–1	1–2	0	1	1
TOTAL	51–90	26–38	48	28	129

3-Point Goals: 1–2 (Free 1–2)

LOS ANGELES

Player	FG-FGA	FT-FTA	Reb.	Ass.	Pts.
Rambis	1–4	0–2	6	1	2
Worthy	8–13	4–5	3	1	20
Abdul-Jabbar	7–18	3–4	4	2	17
Johnson	8–13	7–8	8	8	23
Scott	4–11	1–1	2	2	10
Cooper	3–11	0–0	5	8	9
Lucas	2–8	3–4	4	2	7
Kupchak	2–6	1–2	5	0	5
McGee	1–4	0–0	1	0	2
Green	3–6	0–0	3	1	6
Spriggs	4–8	2–2	2	1	10
TOTAL	43–102	21–28	43	26	111

3-Point Goals: 4–8 (Cooper 3–4, Scott 1–2, McGee 0–1, Green 0–1)

Attendance: 17,505

CAVALIERS 98, NEW JERSEY NETS 89
APRIL 30, 1992

Shedding the Monkey

Tension was beginning to creep into the Cavs' locker room. In seemingly the blink of an eye, a season so promising, so satisfying, now threatened to go up in smoke just as so many before it.

After matching a franchise-best fifty-seven-win regular season, the Cavs looked as if they'd have no trouble with the New Jersey Nets in their best-of-five first-round series. After a pair of crisp wins in Richfield, the Cavaliers headed to the Meadowlands to close out the sixth-seeded Nets. And with a ten-point lead with just over six minutes to play in Game Three, Cleveland's first playoff series victory in sixteen years seemed a done deal. But New Jersey rallied for a five-point win to force Game Four, and suddenly the cruising Cavs were vulnerable. Leading scorer Brad Daugherty was nursing a sore ankle and sparkplug Mark Price was slumping, missing all seven three-point shots he attempted in Game Three. Even worse, the ordinarily sound Cavs had committed a whopping twenty-three turnovers in the loss and given new life to a team that had previously lost ten straight postseason games.

Even worse, specters of past Cavs' failures now began to ooze into the picture. Three times in the previous four seasons, the Cavaliers had clawed to within one victory of a first-round win, and three times they'd been denied. All the accomplishments of a dynamite season were now hanging in the balance as the suddenly confident Nets had all the momentum.

And everything that went wrong in the last six minutes of Game Three continued at the start of Game Four. New Jersey roared to a fifteen-point lead in the early going as the Cavs looked listless and lethargic. With a quarter-inch of tape securing his ankle, Daugherty was struggling, and the Nets were having their way down low, led by brute forward Derrick Coleman. Cleveland stopped the bleeding and narrowed the margin to eight at the half, but the uninviting prospect of returning to the Coliseum for a deciding Game Five two days later loomed like storm clouds on the horizon.

The Nets answered every Cavs' challenge in the third quarter and led by six going into the fourth. Then, with the game on the line, the Cavaliers simply decided they were fed up with the memory of past first-round failures. Daugherty suddenly became a factor underneath, leading a defensive charge that forced the New Jersey offense into reverse. Hobbling on his faulty ankle, Daugherty still ripped down fourteen rebounds. "To see him going got me going, too," Hot Rod Williams said later. Following Daugherty's lead, Williams racked up thirteen boards, as did Larry Nance. And when Williams scored on a layup with 8:15 remaining, the Cavaliers took their first lead of the night at 76–75. But they weren't out of the woods yet.

Trailing by one, Daugherty came in off the bench and made the play of the day—blocking a Coleman shot to keep Cleveland up three with three minutes left. Just over a minute later, Williams hit two clutch free throws, then Craig Ehlo stroked a twenty-footer to put the Cavs up eight and put the final nail in the Nets' coffin. When the buzzer sounded, the Cavaliers had scored a 98–89 win, one of the grittiest in franchise history, and a well-earned trip to the Eastern Conference semifinals. "We hung together," Lenny Wilkens said. "We deserve this."

The recent disappointments were gone forever. "We got the monkey off Cleveland's back," a sore Daugherty said in the locker room. "Even with a broken leg, that would feel good." Williams echoed the sentiment: "We've had a lot of disappointments in the past, but this one wipes them out."

With their win in the Meadowlands, the Cavaliers had written a new chapter in team history, which would begin against the Boston Celtics in what would become a memorable seven-game series.

"The pressure's off," Price said. "Now we can have some fun."

	1	2	3	4	
Cavaliers	16	24	27	31	=98
Nets	30	18	25	16	=89

CLEVELAND

Player	FG-FGA	FT-FTA	Reb.	Ass.	Pts.
Nance	8–19	0–0	13	0	16
Sanders	5–9	1–2	5	2	11
Daugherty	4–12	11–13	14	2	19
Ehlo	5–10	0–0	5	7	11
Price	5–12	6–7	4	3	16
Williams	5–11	10–12	13	2	20
Kerr	1–3	0–0	0	0	3
Battle	1–4	0–0	1	2	2
TOTAL	34–80	28–34	55	18	98

3-Point Goals: 2–5 (Ehlo 1–1, Kerr 1–1, Price 0–3)

NEW JERSEY

Player	FG-FGA	FT-FTA	Reb.	Ass.	Pts.
Morris	8–19	5–6	5	3	22
Coleman	7–21	8–11	14	6	22
Bowie	3–5	3–4	5	4	10
Petrovic	6–14	2–2	0	2	14
Blaylock	4–13	0–0	5	5	8
George	2–5	0–0	0	0	4
Dudley	1–4	3–6	7	0	5
Mills	2–8	0–0	7	1	4
Anderson	0–0	0–0	0	0	0
Lee	0–1	0–0	0	0	0
TOTAL	33–90	21–29	43	21	89

3-Point Goals: 2–11 (Bowie 1–2, Morris 1–4, Coleman 0–1, Petrovic 0–1, Blaylock 0–1, Mills 0–1, Lee 0–1)

Attendance: 13,071

#20

CAVALIERS 114, NEW YORK KNICKS 92
MARCH 24, 1974

Out With the Old

For their first four seasons, the Cleveland Cavaliers reflected the rickety old building they called home: uninviting and, for the most part, ugly. Built in 1937, Cleveland Arena was hardly the ideal forum for a professional sports team. On the outside, it looked like a mausoleum planted right in the heart of a miserable neighborhood. Things were even worse inside, with a warped playing floor spread beneath dim, dangling light fixtures and rats scurrying through the archaic locker rooms and corridors.

Needless to say, the Cavs were eyeing the start of the 1974–75 season like little kids waiting for Christmas morning. That's when they'd bid goodbye to the Arena and move into Nick Mileti's palatial Coliseum nestled in the meadows in Richfield. Unlike the Indians' final days at Cleveland Stadium two decades later, there was little emotion or attention surrounding the Cavs' final countdown at the Arena. As it happened, even fewer fans attended games at the Arena that year than the year before. Yet quietly, the Cavaliers had begun to leave their mark on the warehouse of horrors on Euclid Avenue. Though the 1973–74 Cavs would wind up losing three more games than they had the previous year, they leveled off over the final month of the season. Most notably, they ticked off five straight home victories and actually carried momentum into the Arena finale—a Sunday matinee against the defending world champion New York Knicks.

More than 8,000 fans filed through the rusty turnstiles, comprising one of the bigger Cavs crowds at the Arena, which had averaged just over 4,000 fans per game that season. "The guys will have a little more pride out there playing in front of some people," guard Lenny Wilkens said. Though Cleveland's Bingo Smith noted later it seemed like 3,000 of the fans were the usual Cavs faithful while the other 5,000 were there to see the Knicks—who were looking to secure their second straight fifty-win season.

Those 5,000 fans were pleased in the early going. After the Cavs honored retiring New York forward Dave DeBusschere before the game, presenting him with a plaque and portable television set, the Knicks sprinted out to a seven-point lead. But in the second quarter, Cleveland turned the tables, exploding for thirty-nine points to take a six-point advantage to the half.

As the home team stretched the lead with an equally dazzling third quarter, the loyalty of the crowd began to shift. In addition to the die-hard 3,000 cheering their hearts out as always, many of the others began to jump on the bandwagon and root for the home team. "It changed in the second half," Smith said, "and it will change even more when we get into the new place."

With a home crowd rocking behind them, the Cavs surged to a twenty-point lead and never let the Knicks back in it. The final was 114–92—the Cavaliers' sixth straight victory at the Arena to close out its dubious history. "We'll take those six wins over to the new place," Bill Fitch said. "Beating the world champions is a nice way to go out of the old building."

Naturally, much of the talk afterward centered on the future, specifically Richfield Coliseum. "We're all looking forward to the building," Cleveland forward Steve Patterson said, "and if we can pick up next fall where we leave off, everything will be just fine when we move in."

As it happened, the strong finish to the 1973–74 season, completed by the New York romp in the home finale, did indeed set the tone for the future. The Cavs would win twenty-nine home games in their first season at the Coliseum, notching their first home winning record. And a year after that, they would redefine home-court advantage.

	1	2	3	4	
Knicks	29	26	19	18	=92
Cavaliers	22	39	29	24	=114

NEW YORK

Player	FG-FGA	FT-FTA	Reb.	Ass.	Pts.
DeBusschere	8–13	4–6	4	1	20
Bradley	4–8	3–4	5	3	11
Reed	4–8	3–4	6	1	11
Meminger	2–5	2–2	2	2	6
Monroe	4–9	3–4	4	4	11
Lucas	4–11	0–0	5	3	8
Bibby	4–12	0–2	7	3	8
Jackson	4–6	1–2	6	1	9
Wingo	0–3	4–4	3	0	4
Davis	2–5	0–0	4	1	4
TOTAL	36–80	20–28	46	19	92

CLEVELAND

Player	FG-FGA	FT-FTA	Reb.	Ass.	Pts.
Smith	8–14	3–4	2	1	19
Davis	7–13	1–4	8	3	15
Patterson	3–8	0–0	8	0	6
Carr	6–12	2–2	3	2	14
Wilkens	9–17	4–5	6	11	22
Brewer	3–9	0–0	5	1	6
Cleamons	5–6	2–3	3	3	12
Witte	4–8	0–0	3	1	8
Clemens	3–4	0–0	3	1	6
Warren	2–2	0–0	1	0	4
Foster	1–1	0–0	0	0	2
TOTAL	51–94	12–18	42	23	114

Attendance: 8,829

CAVALIERS 114, NEW JERSEY NETS 100
APRIL 9, 1985

Miracle Part II

The Cavaliers had endured some lean times during their fifteen years of existence, most notably two sixty-seven-loss seasons and nine campaigns of fifty or more losses. But for all the horrors the Cavs had put their fans through, perhaps none was more painful than the start of the 1984–85 season. Over the campaign's first six weeks, Cleveland's seven-year itch turned into full-blown psoriasis.

The dark ages of the Ted Stepien era had officially passed and Cleveland was supposed to be in a rebuilding mode, taking steps back toward reaching the playoffs after nearly a decade hiatus. Instead, the Cavs collapsed out of the starting gate, losing their first nine games for the first time since their expansion season, and by mid-December they stood at a horrific 2–19. For all the changes on and off the court, the Cavs were just as embarrassing as ever.

But ever so slowly, things began to turn around. After playing .500 ball for two months, the Cavs set forth on a spring to remember. A six-game winning streak—including five on a West Coast swing—pushed the Cavaliers into playoff contention in early March. Then, after a three-game losing streak seemed to deflate their hopes two weeks later, the Cavs ripped off six more wins to put themselves on the doorstep of a playoff berth with four games to play. With nine players averaging at least seven points per game and the explosive offensive punch of flamboyant guard World B. Free, the Cavs had transformed into an entirely different team.

Holding a two-game lead over Atlanta, Cleveland had a chance to clinch with a home victory against the playoff-bound New Jersey Nets, who had smashed the Cavs by twenty points three weeks earlier. But with a crowd of better than 10,000 there to witness what just a few months ago seemed like an impossibility, the Cavs fell behind by ten at the half and trailed by as many as fourteen. The playoffs once again looked as far away as they did in November.

But just as it had in this improbable turnaround, the tide turned. In the final three minutes of the third quarter, Cleveland trimmed the ten-point deficit to two but then fell back behind by seven. Once again, the Cavs rallied. Phil Hubbard tipped in a Ben Poquette miss to cut the margin back to two with 6:29 remaining, then center Roy Hinson ripped down one of his eight fourth-quarter rebounds and fed Hubbard for a fast break layup to tie the game. Moments later, Free hit one of his trademark rainbow jumpers to give the Cavs a 97–95 lead. As the ball cleared the net, Free—who would score thirty-five points on the night—pumped his fist into the air, inciting the crowd to decibel levels that shook the building and rekindled memories of the unforgettable 1976 playoff run. Adding even more meaning to the moment, Free hit the shot over Ron Brewer, whom the Cavs traded for Free in 1982.

Cleveland wouldn't trail again and won going away, 114–100. And that triumph, combined with an Atlanta loss in Washington that night, punched the ticket. After seven miserable seasons, the Cleveland Cavaliers were back in the playoffs—and they'd done it by overcoming one of the worst starts in league history. It was easy to forget, backup guard Johnny Davis reminded reporters after the game, that at one point early in the season the Cavs weren't expected to win ten games. "A whole lot of teams would roll over and die," Poquette said, "wouldn't even care, if they were 2–19."

After the team departed the floor following the final buzzer, the Coliseum crowd demanded a curtain call. After the players returned, they hoisted head coach George Karl onto their shoulders and carried him off the floor. "It's a good basketball team," said Stan Albeck, former Cavs' coach now leading New Jersey, "and I think everyone in the league is aware it's not the same Cavs."

Indeed it wasn't. Bill Livingston called it the "Miracle of Richfield II." After the game, Cavs' assistant coach Mo McHone said, "Ever since I came to Cleveland, I've heard about the Miracle of Richfield. Taking nothing away from those guys, but this is the real Miracle of Richfield." Fueling the fire were whispers coming from Boston, where the defending champion Celtics admitted they'd rather play Chicago or Washington than the red-hot upstarts. "The Cavs worrying the Celtics?" Livingston asked. "If that's not enough to qualify as miraculous, what is?"

True, the Cavs only wound up with a 36–46 record, but their 34–27 finish, capped by their symbolic comeback victory over New Jersey, would become one of the defining moments in franchise history. "You don't talk about things like this," Karl said. "You enjoy it for the moment. These guys have done a special thing in the NBA."

	1	2	3	4	
Nets	26	36	23	15	=100
Cavaliers	29	23	31	31	=114

NEW JERSEY

Player	FG-FGA	FT-FTA	Reb.	Ass.	Pts.
Turner	6–10	2–2	4	1	14
Williams	3–9	2–2	2	1	8
Dawkins	2–3	5–6	4	0	9
Ransey	2–10	0–0	2	6	4
Richardson	15–24	2–2	4	11	33
Brewer	7–13	0–0	2	0	14
King	3–10	2–3	1	0	8
Gminski	2–8	6–6	7	3	10
Sappleton	0–2	0–0	4	0	0
TOTAL	40–89	19–21	30	22	100

3-Point Goals: Richardson

CLEVELAND

Player	FG-FGA	FT-FTA	Reb.	Ass.	Pts.
Hubbard	8–10	6–8	4	1	22
Hinson	5–11	3–5	8	1	13
West	0–0	0–0	2	0	0
Bagley	2–4	6–6	3	9	10
Free	13–24	8–10	5	7	35
Davis	4–8	2–4	1	7	11
Shelton	3–8	2–4	7	1	8
Poquette	3–10	4–4	7	0	10
Williams	0–0	0–0	1	1	0
Jones	2–6	1–2	3	0	5
Turpin	0–0	0–0	0	0	0
TOTAL	40–81	32–43	41	27	114

3-Point Goals: Free, Davis

Attendance: 10,185

CAVALIERS 114, BOSTON CELTICS 112 (OT)
MAY 10, 1992

Larry Legend

Before LeBron James, before Kobe Bryant, even before Michael Jordan, professional basketball was symbolized by a lanky, blonde-haired farm boy from French Lick, Indiana. Larry Bird's heroics not only redefined the greatness of the Boston Celtics franchise in the 1980s but also catapulted the NBA into a realm of popularity it had never seen before.

By 1992, Bird's illustrious career was drawing to a close. Nagging injuries had taken their toll and the future Hall of Famer could no longer dominate a game like he once could. Likewise, perennial All-Star teammates Kevin McHale and Robert Parish were aging as well, and the Celtics were trying to balance introducing a new generation of players while still cashing in on the experience of their veterans.

Even without Bird, out nursing a back injury, the Celtics had the Cavaliers on the ropes in the 1992 playoffs. After Cleveland rolled to victory in the first game of their best-of-seven semifinal series, Boston bounced back to win the next two and was poised to take a choke hold on the series. They'd host Game Four at Boston Garden on Mother's Day, and with a victory, the Celts would be on the brink of advancing to the Eastern Conference finals for the first time in four years. The Cavs, meanwhile, were trying not to let their magical fifty-seven-win season quietly fizzle out. But in order to extend their magic, they'd have to overcome some.

After sitting out fourteen straight games, Bird would return to action in Game Four before an adoring Garden crowd—the 540th consecutive sellout at the old basketball museum atop Boston's North Station. It promised to be an emotional afternoon for Bird and the Celtics, who were already rolling, winning thirteen of the fourteen games Bird missed and twenty in a row at the Garden. For the Cavs, it had all the makings of a recipe for disaster.

Sure enough, the Garden foundation rumbled when Bird entered the game and hit his first shot—a twenty-footer midway through the second quarter. But the Cavs withstood the tidal wave of emotion and pulled away before the half, parlaying a 68 percent shooting clip in the second quarter to a twelve-point lead. The margin swelled to fourteen points midway through the third, when the Celtics cued up some of their usual Garden magic.

With young forward Reggie Lewis leading a scoring onslaught that would result in a career-high forty-two points, Boston cut the lead to three going into the fourth. "Guarding him," Brad Daugherty said, "is becoming a lot like guarding Michael Jordan." The teams jousted back and forth through an epic fourth quarter, each knowing whoever won would be in the driver's seat for the series. Former Cav John Bagley hit a twelve-footer to put Boston up 103–99 with 1:16 to play, but Mark Price responded with a driving bucket. Then, when Parish went up for a game-clinching dunk with thirty seconds left, Larry Nance and Hot Rod Williams combined to reject the shot and give the Cavs new life. Seconds later, Williams tied the game with a pair of free throws. Then, finally, Cleveland appeared poised to take victory when Nance grabbed a clutch rebound of a Lewis miss and Williams was sent to the line with 8.2 seconds left and the score tied at 103. But Williams, who had made ten consecutive free throws, missed both shots and suddenly the Celtics had a chance to win. Lewis missed a fifteen-footer at the buzzer and the teams plunged into overtime.

In the extra session, it was the game's other Larry who rose to the occasion. The Cavs' Nance was already enjoying a career game. Not only had he smothered Bird defensively, Nance would hit thirteen of sixteen shots—including three in overtime—for thirty-two points to go with seven rebounds. Yet when Nance had an open look from sixteen feet with the Cavs up one with thirty seconds left, he passed up the shot and fired the ball to a wide-open Daugherty for a layup that made it 113–110. "Wasn't that beautiful?" Lenny Wilkens said afterward. "That was basketball." Yet the Cavaliers weren't in the clear.

After Boston scored to cut the lead to one, Daugherty missed the first of two free throws, which could have kept the Cavs in control with 14.7 seconds remaining. He hit the second to put Cleveland up two, but the Celtics would have one more chance—and in came Bird off the bench. With the clock ticking down under five seconds, Larry Legend took a pass from Lewis and drove to the basket but missed a running layup. Lewis grabbed the rebound and tossed up an awkward shot from ten feet that didn't hit anything. The ball bounced out of the key as time expired, and the Cavs had secured an immense playoff victory on the road.

They'd outlasted the seasoned Celtics on an emotional afternoon in the toughest arena in basketball and knotted the series at two games apiece. Cavs' general manager Wayne Embry called it the biggest victory since he'd come to Cleveland, while Bill Livingston noted, "As miracles go, this one rivals Richfield, 1976."

There were plenty of heroes for the victors—Price scored twenty-six and dished out twelve assists, Daugherty added twenty points, Williams eighteen, and scrappy Craig Ehlo missed all nine shots he took but managed to rip down an uncharacteristic nine rebounds. But the difference maker was Larry Nance, who saved the Cavs' season by dominating the game the way Bird used to.

That afternoon, Bird had to share the moniker "Larry Legend."

	1	2	3	4	OT	
Cavaliers	26	37	20	20	11	=114
Celtics	27	24	29	23	9	=112

CLEVELAND

Player	FG-FGA	FT-FTA	Reb.	Ass.	Pts.
Nance	13–16	6–6	7	2	32
Sanders	3–6	3–4	2	1	9
Daugherty	9–15	2–2	8	1	20
Ehlo	0–9	1–2	9	3	1
Price	11–18	2–4	2	12	26
Williams	4–11	10–12	7	4	18
Brandon	3–3	0–0	1	2	6
Battle	0–1	2–2	0	0	2
TOTAL	43–79	26–32	36	25	114

3-Point Goals: 2–8 (Price 2–5, Ehlo 0–3)

BOSTON

Player	FG-FGA	FT-FTA	Reb.	Ass.	Pts.
Gamble	2–6	0–0	3	2	4
Pinckney	5–7	0–0	9	2	10
Parish	7–16	2–3	18	1	16
Bagley	3–10	2–2	3	7	8
Lewis	16–28	9–12	3	6	42
McHale	8–15	7–9	5	1	23
Brown	1–4	0–0	0	5	2
Bird	1–5	2–2	2	3	4
Fox	1–1	0–0	0	0	3
TOTAL	44–92	22–28	43	27	112

3-Point Goals: 2–4 (Lewis 1–1, Fox 1–1, Pinckney 0–1, Bird 0–1)

Attendance: 14,890

#17

With a Little Help From Their Friends

It didn't seem to matter that the Cavs had lost the first two games of the Eastern Conference finals, nor that they were now just two defeats away from extinction. Both the Cavs and the favored Boston Celtics knew the series was about to take a dramatic turn. After Boston had eked out a pair of narrow victories at the Garden, the teams would head west to the Cavs' friendly palace of decibels within Richfield Coliseum. Even Celtics' coach Tommy Heinsohn refused to be optimistic when asked about his squad's chances in the third and fourth games. "They will have all their friends with them," he said of the Cavaliers.

To be precise, the Cavs would have 21,564 friends in their corner, ready to scream themselves hoarse as they willed their beloved team to victory. Almost overnight, Richfield, Ohio, had become the last place in the world any basketball team but the Cleveland Cavaliers wanted to play. Yet for all the excitement, all was not right in Cavs nation. Head coach Bill Fitch and owner Nick Mileti were squabbling through the media, Mileti claiming Fitch had asked out of his contract to cash in his Cleveland success to become the head coach of the Los Angeles Lakers. Fitch denied it, but a coolness had settled over the team, and some wondered if it might affect its play.

Just as had been the case throughout the conference semifinals, the Coliseum was packed well before tip-off on a Wednesday night and the fans were charged and ready for action, some brandishing signs reading, "If Fitch Goes, We Go." The Cavs' coach, who would officially be named the NBA's Coach of the Year later that week, received a standing ovation when he took the floor. Despite whatever was going on between him and Mileti, the adoring Cleveland faithful appreciated everything Fitch had done in guiding the team from an expansion laughingstock to the brink of a championship. "God bless those fans," Fitch said. "I've never been in a more emotional situation."

And as they had all spring, the players took a cue from their fans. The Cava-liers came out sharp, charging to a 12–2 lead while committing only two turnovers in the first half and a mere seven for the game. Meanwhile the Cleveland defense suffocated the Celtics, stifling star forward John Havlicek into a four-for-fourteen shooting performance after he'd scored a combined forty-six points in the first two games of the series. Forward Paul Silas hit just three of eleven, and center Dave Cowens, smothered by Nate Thurmond, connected on just eight of eighteen. The thirty-four-year-old Thurmond was playing with the energy of a rookie, taking in stride the additional minutes he'd inherited when starting center Jim Chones went down prior to the series with a broken foot. With Thurmond anchoring the unit down low, the Cavs' defense was simply incredible. Boston, which had averaged 104 points in its eight previous playoff games, was held to thirty-eight in the first half and seventy-eight for the game— a Cleveland playoff record. Offensively, the Cavs were paced by guard Austin Carr, who put it all together for the first time in a long time, scoring seventeen points in just twenty-five minutes of play off the bench.

With the game tied at sixty-two early in the fourth, Cleveland began to pull away. Jim Brewer tipped in a miss, then Carr nailed a pair of free throws, and Bingo Smith drilled a long jumper to put the Cavs up six. Appropriately, a twenty-eight-foot jump shot by Carr put the Cavs up 80–72 with a minute left and put the stake in Boston's heart. "We didn't play the game like we were down 2–0," Fitch said. "We played it like the seventh game." The Coliseum crowd rose its game to another level as well. "You might say there's no way they can get louder," Fitch said. "I've said that five or six times myself. But wait 'til Friday. They'll be louder."

The 83–78 triumph also softened the animosity between coach and owner. Mileti approached Fitch in the locker room afterward. "Nice going, Billy," he said. "Thanks," Fitch replied, and Mileti left. The resolution to their conflict would come another day, but on this cool May evening, hard feelings and self-doubt took a back seat to Cavalier magic.

	1	2	3	4	
Celtics	16	22	16	24	=78
Cavaliers	16	27	15	25	=83

BOSTON

Player	FG-FGA	FT-FTA	Reb.	Ass.	Pts.
Havlicek	4–14	1–1	8	0	9
Silas	3–11	6–6	21	1	12
Cowens	8–18	3–5	20	3	19
White	11–26	0–2	7	7	22
Scott	4–17	0–0	3	1	8
Stacom	0–2	0–0	2	0	0
Nelson	1–2	2–2	1	0	4
Kuberski	1–3	2–2	1	1	4
Aro	0–0	0–0	0	1	0
McDonald	0–0	0–0	0	0	0
TOTAL	32–93	14–18	63	14	78

CLEVELAND

Player	FG-FGA	FT-FTA	Reb.	Ass.	Pts.
Smith	7–18	0–0	4	1	14
Brewer	2–7	2–2	15	4	6
Thurmond	3–10	0–0	9	6	6
Snyder	2–11	1–2	3	2	5
Cleamons	8–14	2–2	9	3	18
Russell	5–15	4–4	3	2	14
Witte	1–1	0–0	0	1	2
Carr	7–15	3–5	1	1	17
Walker	0–1	1–2	0	0	1
TOTAL	35–92	13–17	44	20	83

Attendance: 21,564

#16

CAVALIERS 73, CHICAGO BULLS 70
FEBRUARY 27, 1997

Incredi-Bull

It was hard enough for the Cavs to watch the Chicago Bulls win three straight NBA titles in the early 1990s since they knew they were likely the second-best team in basketball through much of the Bulls' reign. Twice Michael Jordan had ended Cleveland's season with buzzer-beating, playoff-clinching shots, and countless times in between he'd carved through the Cavaliers to forty-, fifty-, and even sixty-point performances. Even when Jordan abruptly retired in 1993, the Cavs stayed one step behind the Bulls, who continued to contend for a title. But when Jordan's return to basketball coincided with the maturity of star forward Scottie Pippen and the acquisition of extraterrestrial but talented rebound machine Dennis Rodman, the Bulls of the late 1990s were even better than they'd been before.

Chicago rolled to an incredible 72–10 record in the 1995–96 season, the NBA's best ever, capturing the first of what would once again become three consecutive championships. And as the 1996–97 campaign entered its final third, the Bulls were just as dominant, holding a 49–6 mark on the second-to-last day of February. Overall, including the playoffs, Chicago had won 136 of its last 156 games. Not surprisingly, they had swept past the Cavaliers six straight times, typically in lopsided fashion, leading Bill Livingston to opine, "The Bulls seem not to be merely a different style from the Cavs. They are a different civilization."

The 30–24 Cavaliers were solid but still appeared no match for the mighty Bulls, who had won seven straight games—the last five by an average of better than nineteen points per contest. And the streak had been put together without Rodman, who'd served an eleven-game suspension for kicking a courtside cameraman during a game. Averaging thirteen rebounds per contest and sporting his fourth different hair color of the season, Rodman would return to action at Gund Arena. Conversely, the Cavs would be without their leading rebounder, Tyrone Hill, who was out with a sprained ankle.

Yet from the opening tip, the Cavs managed to take the Bulls out of their usual flow. Parlaying a suffocating defense, Cleveland held Chicago to just fourteen points in the first quarter as the home team charged to a nine-point halftime lead. Jordan and Pippen were both being contained and every Chicago shot was being contested. Just the third sellout crowd of the season was roaring as the underdog Cavs continued to control the game through the third quarter, at one point leading by sixteen points. But, as expected, Jordan and Company came charging back in the fourth, sparking a 15–2 run to cut the margin to three and swing the momentum.

The Cavs needed someone to step up to turn the tide back in their favor. And to everyone's surprise, the hero came in the form of a Ukrainian rookie center from Wright State University named Vitaly Potapenko. Used sparingly during the season thus far and averaging just over five points per game, Potapenko caught fire, hitting all four of his shots from the field and scoring twelve points in the critical fourth quarter. Yet despite Potapenko's heroics, the Bulls were right in the mix in the waning seconds.

After a turnover by the Cavs' Danny Ferry, Pippen nailed a pair of free throws to cut the Cleveland lead to 72–70 with 19.7 seconds left. With ten seconds showing, Cleveland forward Chris Mills hit one of two free throws to put the Cavs up three, but it left the door open just a crack for Michael Jordan, who'd made a career out of breaking Cleveland's heart. "Any time he has the ball in his hands," Cavs' guard Terrell Brandon said later, "you cross your fingers and hope for the best."

During the ensuing timeout, Pippen waltzed over to Jordan. "You gonna do it again?" Pippen asked. "Why not?" Jordan replied.

Sure enough, Jordan got the ball, and with time running out, he launched an off-balanced twenty-eight-foot jumper that would have tied the game. It hit the rim and rattled around the cylinder for seemingly an eternity before rolling off and into the waiting hands of Brandon. The buzzer sounded and the Cavaliers had handed the Bulls one of just thirteen losses they'd suffer on the season. Cleveland had crippled the Chicago offense, limiting the Bulls to season lows in points scored, field goals made, field goal percentage, and three-point percentage. Jordan, ferociously guarded by Bobby Phills all night, hit just seven of his twenty-five shots and was held to a very human twenty-three points. "We didn't want to play that type of game with them," Pippen said, "but that's the style of play they lure you into."

Perhaps more stunning than the Cavs' defensive shutdown, for the first time in memory, Jordan was unable to come through with the game on the line, enabling the Cavaliers to knock off the Chicago Bulls. That alone made the victory one of the most satisfying—and memorable—in Cavs' history.

	1	2	3	4	
Bulls	14	18	20	18	=70
Cavaliers	21	20	21	11	=73

CHICAGO

Player	FG-FGA	FT-FTA	Reb.	Ass.	Pts.
Pippen	5–13	4–6	14	2	14
Rodman	6–11	4–4	16	1	16
Longley	3–5	0–0	2	0	6
Harper	1–8	0–0	2	1	2
Jordan	7–25	9–9	8	4	23
Kukoc	1–6	2–4	3	2	4
Caffey	1–2	0–0	1	1	2
Kerr	1–4	0–1	2	1	3
Buechler	0–0	0–0	0	0	0
Brown	0–2	0–0	0	0	0
TOTAL	25–76	19–24	48	12	70

3-point goals: 1–14 (Kerr 1–3, Kukoc 0–2, Harper 0–2, Jordan 0–3, Pippen 0–4)

CLEVELAND

Player	FG-FGA	FT-FTA	Reb.	Ass.	Pts.
Mills	3–9	1–2	5	3	7
Ferry	4–12	0–0	7	2	9
West	2–3	1–2	4	1	5
Brandon	9–20	5–5	5	5	23
Phills	5–14	0–0	7	3	13
Potapenko	5–7	2–2	5	0	12
Sura	0–0	1–2	3	5	1
Marshall	1–2	0–0	0	0	3
TOTAL	29–67	10–13	36	19	73

3-Point Goals: 5–15 (Phills 3–4, Marshall 1–1, Ferry 1–4, Mills 0–2, Brandon 0–4)

Attendance: 20,562

#15

CAVALIERS 105, BOSTON CELTICS 98
APRIL 23, 1985

Mixing Magic

Since no one—not even themselves—had expected the Cavaliers to come this far this fast, the entire city was beaming with sudden, surprising pride. After four straight seasons of fifty or more losses, then a miserable 2–19 start, the Cavs had turned around their 1984–85 season and the entire franchise by earning their first playoff berth in seven years.

Granted, everybody knew the experience wouldn't last long. In the first round, Cleveland was paired with defending champ Boston, fueled by Larry Bird, Kevin McHale, and Robert Parish in their primes. The Cavs were hot but stood little chance against the finest team in basketball, which had defeated Cleveland a whopping fifteen straight times. "Let us not kid ourselves," the *Plain Dealer*'s Bob Dolgan wrote. "The Cavs are not loaded with talent. But every once in a while, the moon shines right and a club in a team game mixes magic and chemistry and makes everything turn out right."

Dolgan very nearly called it. In the face of overwhelming logic, the upstart Cavaliers stood up to the league bully and threw a huge scare into the Celtics. Despite forty points from Bird in Game One at Boston Garden, Boston's 126–123 victory wasn't secured until World B. Free's three-point shot at the buzzer rattled out. On a Saturday afternoon two days later, the Cavs came even closer. Before a national audience—marking Cleveland's first appearance on network TV in almost six years—the Cavs rallied from a thirteen-point third-quarter deficit to battle through a nip-and-tuck fourth quarter. Once again, the Celtics escaped when a potentially game-tying, twenty-five-foot shot by Free was off the mark at the buzzer. Boston led the best-of-five series two games to none, but the Cavs had proven to be anything but pushovers.

For Game Three, the scene shifted to Richfield Coliseum, which had become the epicenter of the celebration. "It's going to be the biggest basketball night of the year," Dolgan wrote. "The noise will be so loud, it will make your hair hurt. What fun it will be." With red-and-white bunting adorning the concourses, the Coliseum would be packed to the rafters with a capacity crowd that included Ohio Governor Richard Celeste, Cleveland Mayor George Voinovich, and NBA Commissioner David Stern. More important than who was there was who wasn't. After playing a combined ninety minutes in the first two games, Larry Bird would sit out the third game with bone chips in his elbow. Though prior to the series, it seemed the Celtics would cruise to victory with or without Bird, now his absence meant much more.

With the Coliseum crowd rocking behind them, the Cavs grabbed a 4–2 lead and never looked back. They rolled to a fourteen-point advantage late in the first half and then carried a ten-point margin into the fourth quarter, when the shorthanded Celtics made their charge. Led by Scott Wedman, who filled in for Bird and wound up with thirty points, Boston scored the first eight points of the period to cut the margin to two. But the Cavs managed to keep the defending champions at arm's length. Leading 92–90, Cleveland forward Roy Hinson hit a twelve-foot turnaround jumper with 2:49 left to begin the Cavs' pull-away. A three-point play by Free—who was having a marvelous game—with a minute remaining put Cleveland up eight, and the party began. In the final seconds, the African hunger-relief anthem "We Are the World" played over the speakers in homage to the Cavs' dynamic guard, and the sellout crowd sang along.

After struggling in the first two games in Boston, Free caught fire in Game Three, scoring thirty-two points and dishing out eight assists. But he wasn't the only hero. Guard John Bagley collected fifteen assists, a franchise playoff record, while Hinson rang up twenty-one points and nine rebounds in just twenty-eight minutes of action.

As the clock ticked down, the crowd began to chant, "We Want Bird!" Dolgan called the victory over the Bird-less Celtics "like outrunning a three-legged man," but the Cavs would take it. "Give us some compliments," Free said afterward. "Are we supposed to roll over and die because Bird was out?"

Considering they'd somehow shrugged off an embarrassing stretch of recent history, then nineteen losses in the first twenty-one games of the season to hold their own against the world champs, rolling over and dying was no longer an option.

	1	2	3	4	
Celtics	24	21	21	32	=98
Cavaliers	25	30	21	29	=105

BOSTON

Player	FG-FGA	FT-FTA	Reb.	Ass.	Pts.
McHale	5–10	11–12	11	1	21
Wedman	13–20	4–6	8	4	30
Parish	9–18	1–2	8	2	19
Johnson	7–19	4–5	6	10	18
Ainge	0–6	0–0	2	2	0
Williams	2–9	0–0	0	7	4
Maxwell	1–5	4–4	6	0	6
Kite	0–0	0–0	0	0	0
Buckner	0–0	0–0	0	0	0
TOTAL	37–87	24–29	41	26	98

3-point goals: 0–4 (Wedman 0–1, Ainge 0–1, Williams 0–2)

CLEVELAND

Player	FG-FGA	FT-FTA	Reb.	Ass.	Pts.
Hubbard	4–10	7–8	4	0	15
Hinson	10–14	1–2	9	1	21
West	0–0	0–2	4	1	0
Bagley	1–10	4–6	7	15	6
Free	13–23	6–6	3	8	32
Shelton	6–8	2–2	5	1	14
Davis	1–3	1–2	1	5	3
Poquette	2–4	0–0	4	0	4
Turpin	5–9	0–0	3	0	10
Anderson	0–1	0–0	1	0	0
Jones	0–1	0–0	1	0	0
TOTAL	42–83	21–28	42	31	105

3-Point Goals: 0–3 (Bagley 0–1, Free 0–1, Davis 0–1)

Attendance: 20,900

CHICAGO BULLS 101, CAVALIERS 100
MAY 7, 1989

Trilogy of Despair

This wasn't supposed to happen. Some couldn't even come to grips with the reality that it had in fact gone this far.

It had been the greatest season in Cavaliers' history, as they exploded from the pack of the mediocre to become the finest team in professional basketball. The Cavs started the 1988–89 campaign winning twenty-one of their first twenty-six games and in early March held the best record in the NBA at 43–12. They were cruising toward not only the Central Division title but, with their success against the defending Eastern Conference champion Detroit Pistons, toward an anticipated trip to the NBA Finals.

Then fate took a cruel turn. Smacked with a handful of nagging injuries, Cleveland only managed to play .500 basketball over the final six weeks of the season, allowing the Pistons to sprint past them for the division title and top playoff seed. Still, the Cavs won a franchise-best fifty-seven games, and, though they were hobbling going into the first round, they were matched with the Chicago Bulls, whom they had utterly dominated all season, winning all six times they'd played. If the Cavs could get healthy and gather some momentum against the Bulls, they still might make good on the once-bright promise of this magical season.

Instead, things only became more implausible. After posting a 37–4 home record during the season, Cleveland lost Game One to the Bulls at Richfield, primarily because Mark Price didn't suit up with a groin injury. That night, the Cavs' focus turned to survival. Price returned to help win Game Two. Then the Cavs were overwhelmed in Game Three in Chicago before clinging to a critical win in the fourth game to send the series back to Richfield for the deciding Game Five. Along the way, Michael Jordan had evolved from a pesky nuisance to the greatest Cavs' killer in team history. Jordan had always enjoyed success against Cleveland, lighting up the Cavs for fifty or more points four times in the previous three years. But in this series, he'd become utterly unstoppable, averaging 38.8 points over the first four games. "Maybe Michael is trying to beat us all by himself," Price wondered after Game Four.

The matchup for Game Five was hopelessly simple. "It is Michael Jordan versus the Cavaliers," the *Plain Dealer*'s Burt Graeff wrote, "and forget all this rubbish about the point-guard-pass-the-ball-around propaganda ground out the last month by the Bulls' publicity department."

It would be the fourth deciding playoff game in Cavs' history, and from the opening tip, it had the feeling of a masterpiece. Playing for the eleventh time on the season, the teams knew each other too well to try to fool one another. On an unseasonably chilly Sunday afternoon, the Bulls and Cavs put on a display better resembling a chess match. The contest would be tied six times and see twenty lead changes—eight in the final 2:30. The capacity crowd watched breathlessly as time and again the Cavaliers were poised to build a comfortable lead, but each time Jordan and the Bulls responded with a run of their own.

Cleveland took a six-point lead into a fourth quarter that would alter the course of history for both franchises. While Jordan propelled the Bulls, the Cavs' hero was unsung Craig Ehlo, who limped in off the bench to play the greatest quarter of his career. After missing the third game with an ankle injury, Ehlo was yet another Cav playing at less than full strength, but he rose to the occasion with a trio of clutch three-pointers in the final twelve minutes. His third wiped out a two-point Chicago lead with fifty-two seconds left and put the Cavs up one, sending the frazzled home crowd into delirium. When Jordan missed a shot on Chicago's ensuing possession, the Cavs had a chance to take control with the clock winding down. But Larry Nance missed a wide-open eighteen-footer with twenty-one seconds left and the Bulls were given new life.

Naturally, Jordan responded with a soaring twelve-foot jumper with six seconds remaining to give Chicago a 99–98 advantage. With their storybook season hanging in the balance, Lenny Wilkens drew up a gem for the ensuing inbound play from midcourt. Ehlo tossed the ball in to Nance and then darted past Craig Hodges. Nance flipped the basketball back to a zooming Ehlo, who went up and ducked under Jordan for the biggest layup in Cleveland history with three seconds left. Once again, the Coliseum crowd exploded, celebrating another huge play by the unassuming Ehlo, who had now scored fifteen points in the fourth quarter and eight of Cleveland's last ten. One more defensive stop and the battered Cavs would live to fight another day.

Everyone in North America knew who would get the ball, and the Cavs were fully prepared. After the teams lined up for the play, Cleveland called time out to make final adjustments. On his way back to the bench, Jordan glanced at Lenny Wilkens and smiled. Nance matched up with Jordan on the inbound pass from Cleveland native Brad Sellers, but Jordan broke free to take the ball on the run. He broke past Nance and found Ehlo waiting for him twenty feet from the basket. Ehlo stayed with the Bulls' superstar stride for stride as the clock ticked down to the final second. Three feet behind the foul stripe, Jordan launched skyward, his momentum still carrying him to his left. Ehlo went up with him, stretching his left hand into Jordan's face. As Ehlo started to come down, Jordan continued to hang in midair, just long enough for Ehlo's hand to clear the basketball's path. Jordan released the ball, and it spun toward the hoop with picture-perfect rotation. Just after the buzzer sounded, the basketball hit the right side of the iron and rattled dramatically through the cylinder—Jordan's forty-third and forty-fourth points of the afternoon.

As Jordan turned and pumped his fist emphatically into the air, Ehlo flung himself into the courtside seats along the sideline. The Coliseum crowd hushed. The magical season was suddenly over, and the Bulls' rise to arguably the greatest team in basketball history had begun. And Cleveland's reputation as a hard-luck sports town was further cemented. "This was a plot the Cavs borrowed from the Browns," Bill Livingston wrote. "The Dog-bone Drive and the Byner fumble. And Michael Jordan's shot. Trilogies of defeat, despair, and disappointment."

The mood in the Cleveland locker room was that of disbelief. "We played him perfectly," Brad Daugherty said. "We had a man in front of him, a man behind him, we jumped at him as he shot and made him change his shot in mid-air, and still . . ." he trailed off. There were no words. Logic itself had been defeated.

"I just can't fathom how in the world our season has ended," Daugherty went on, almost to himself. "Just one man took it to us, all by himself. Amazing. Michael is just amazing."

His legend was just beginning. And Ehlo, whose fourth-quarter heroics had disappeared in a red-and-black poof, would come to personify the futility for all who had tried and would try to stop Michael Jordan. "It'll be tough to live with this one all summer long," Ehlo muttered afterward.

Little did he know they'd be living with it much longer than that.

	1	2	3	4	
Bulls	24	22	23	32	=101
Cavaliers	28	20	27	25	=100

CHICAGO

Player	FG-FGA	FT-FTA	Reb.	Ass.	Pts.
Pippen	4–14	3–8	10	2	13
Grant	6–10	0–0	5	1	12
Cartwright	6–7	4–5	5	1	16
Jordan	17–32	9–13	9	6	44
Hodges	4–12	0–0	2	4	10
Sellers	1–3	0–0	3	3	2
Corzine	1–4	0–0	3	1	2
Vincent	1–1	0–0	0	2	2
Davis	0–0	0–0	0	0	0
TOTAL	40–83	16–26	37	20	101

3-Point Goals: 5–11 (Hodges 2–4, Pippen 2–6, Jordan 1–1)

CLEVELAND

Player	FG-FGA	FT-FTA	Reb.	Ass.	Pts.
Williams	2–5	3–4	6	3	7
Nance	5–11	6–7	7	1	16
Daugherty	3–9	2–2	11	6	8
Harper	9–16	4–5	2	6	22
Price	8–14	4–4	6	7	23
Ehlo	9–15	2–2	2	4	24
Rollins	0–1	0–0	0	0	0
Sanders	0–0	0–0	0	0	0
Valentine	0–0	0–0	0	1	0
TOTAL	36–71	21–24	34	28	100

3-Point Goals: 7–12 (Ehlo 4–7, Price 3–4, Harper 0–1)

Attendance: 20,273

#13

CAVALIERS 105, PORTLAND TRAIL BLAZERS 103
NOVEMBER 12, 1970

The First

Bill Fitch was a haunted, harrowed man.

He couldn't sleep. He couldn't eat. He'd spend his endless, jittery nights camped out in a hotel bar, drinking gallons of coffee and trying to convince himself he hadn't just made the biggest mistake of his life.

For all the quips and one-liners Fitch tossed to reporters, making light of what had become an intolerable situation, he suffered silently, his mind whirling and insides churning. The expansion Cleveland Cavaliers had tried fifteen times to pick up their first win, and fifteen times they had failed.

And in general, they were so hopelessly outmatched that the games quickly became exercises in futility. Over the fifteen-game stretch, the Cavs lost by an average of nineteen points per game, including defeats of thirty, thirty-five, and fifty-four points. Following the fifteenth loss—a 109–74 thumping at the hands of the San Francisco Warriors—the seams of Fitch's sense of humor began to show. "We're just terrible," he said after the Cavs shot a miserable 24 percent from the floor in the loss. "The only way we could beat a team like the Warriors is if Jerry Lucas, Nate Thurmond, and Jeff Mullins all dropped dead. Even then we'd have to play a near-perfect game to beat what's left."

He'd been a successful college coach, rising from tiny Coe College in Cedar Rapids, Iowa, to the University of Minnesota. He'd cashed it in for a shot at the NBA and now wondered if he'd made the right decision. "This isn't going to end," a beleaguered Fitch said at one point. "We're gonna lose some more before we win one. This is tearing my guts out."

Fitch's Cavs were now three defeats away from tying the NBA record for most consecutive losses. And there was no end in sight. "I'm starting to get calls from newspapers all over the country," Fitch said. "If I'm gonna slit my throat, everybody wants me to give them the scoop just before I do it."

Adding insult to injury, the Cavs' fellow expansion company wasn't in quite as much misery. Both the first-year Buffalo Braves and Portland Trail Blazers had managed to win a few games by mid-November and already appeared much further developed than the Cavaliers.

The Cavs seemed to be following the same script on November 12 in Portland, as the Blazers took control of the game early and grabbed a nine-point lead in the third quarter. It was the all-too-familiar point of the contest at which the Cavaliers would fall apart and deliver their sixteenth consecutive loss. Instead, for the first time, the Cavs didn't wither away when the going got tough.

Bolstered by their bench, the Cavaliers fought back with a 9–0 run capped by a game-tying jumper by guard John Warren. Portland surged back ahead by six going into the fourth quarter, but Cleveland stayed close. With three minutes left, forward McCoy McLemore drilled an eighteen-footer to put the Cavs up 97–96, then on the next possession, guard Bobby Lewis hit a jumper to give the Cavs a lead they wouldn't relinquish. Lewis hit three more clutch shots in the final two-and-a-half minutes to secure the victory. Though for a few fleeting moments after the clock hit zero, the issue was still in doubt since the buzzer failed to go off. Considering what the Cavaliers had been through over the past month, it only seemed appropriate.

Ironically, with the 105–103 triumph, Cleveland became the first of the three expansion clubs to win a road game, disappointing a measly crowd of 2,167 at Portland's Memorial Coliseum. For one night at least, the Cavaliers' troubles disappeared. Six players scored in double digits, led by center Walt Wesley's twenty-one points and fifteen rebounds. For the first time, the Cavs outshot an opponent at the foul line and outrebounded them. Bill Fitch's twenty-nine-day nightmare was over.

True, the Cavs were still far from becoming a competitive team. After that night, they would lose twelve more before notching their second victory and would play forty games before winning two straight. But for a few hours, the agony was forgotten.

And Bill Fitch finally got a good night's sleep.

	1	2	3	4	
Cavaliers	28	25	24	28	=105
Trail Blazers	31	26	26	20	=103

CLEVELAND

Player	FG	FT-FTA	Pts.
Smith	1	5–5	7
McLemore	8	3–5	19
Wesley	7	7–10	21
Warren	7	4–5	18
Johnson	6	2–2	14
Lewis	5	2–2	12
Egan	1	0–0	2
Sorenson	4	4–6	12
Suiter	0	0–0	0
Anderson	0	0–0	0
Cooke	0	0–0	0
TOTAL	39	27–35	105

PORTLAND

Player	FG	FT-FTA	Pts.
Knight	4	1–3	9
Adelman	6	0–0	12
Ellis	1	4–4	6
Barnett	12	3–3	27
Petrie	4	4–10	12
Halimon	2	0–0	4
Schlueter	3	2–4	8
McKenzie	7	9–12	23
Manning	1	0–0	2
TOTAL	40	23–36	103

Attendance: 2,173

#12

Bingo!

In the Cavaliers' first-ever playoff game they looked very much like a team that was playing its first-ever playoff game. Taking on the seasoned Washington Bullets, who had reached the NBA Finals the year before, the Cavs had been overwhelmed on their home court in Game One of their 1976 Eastern Conference semifinal series, trailing by twenty-one points at the half in what became a 100–95 defeat. Though the Cavaliers had leap-frogged Washington to capture the Central Division title, most expected the Bullets would handle Cleveland in the playoffs and atone for what they felt was a regular season of underachievement.

If experience was the key to postseason success, then the Cavaliers were in trouble. "The biggest weakness the Cavaliers have in this series is that they never have been through one before," *Plain Dealer* sports editor Hal Lebovitz wrote in the aftermath of the first game. "It's a pressure they never coped with. They don't know if they can. They're uncertain."

Accordingly, Cleveland players and coaches spent the next forty-eight hours trying to keep panic from settling in. "We have six more games," Jim Chones explained, "and if we just play the same ball we did all year, I don't see why we can't win." Bill Fitch simplified it further: "This game doesn't mean a doggone thing if we win in Washington." Yet that would be easier said than done.

Before nearly 18,000 fans at the Capital Centre in Landover, Maryland, the Bullets grabbed a ten-point halftime lead and once again appeared poised to coast to triumph. Cleveland's lackadaisical play in the second quarter reminded Fitch of the "GMA" offense of the early expansion years—"general milling around." But the Cavs fought back. Veteran guard Dick Snyder caught fire in the third quarter, leading an inspired charge back to tie the score.

Momentum seesawed throughout a long, tense fourth quarter. Washington led 79–78 with twenty-nine seconds left when Bingo Smith—the last of the original Cavaliers—was called for traveling, giving the Bullets the ball and a chance to seal victory. With the home crowd buzzing, Washington melted the clock under ten seconds. Then, with six seconds showing, guard Dave Bing was whistled for palming the basketball, and the Cavs were given one last chance. And it was here that Cleveland sports history took an incredible turn.

Jim Cleamons inbounded to Smith, still stinging from his critical turnover twenty-three seconds before. Smith took three dribbles and launched what would become one of the most important shots in Cavalier history. From twenty-seven feet away, the ball splashed through the net with two seconds remaining, giving Cleveland an 80–79 lead. With one fateful swish, Smith had gone from goat to hero and gave the Cavs new life in the series. "Anytime you shoot you have a 50 percent chance it's going in," Smith said, "but I really felt this one was in."

Washington's Elvin Hayes missed a desperation shot at the buzzer and the series was knotted at one game apiece thanks to Smith's miraculous shot. "Bingo!" Bill Nichols wrote in the next morning's *Plain Dealer.* "The Cavaliers are alive and well and all knotted up in their tension-packed playoff series with the Washington Bullets."

Though nobody knew it yet, there was still plenty of tension yet to come. "With the playoff jitters obviously behind them," Chuck Heaton wrote, "the Cavaliers can settle down for what is shaping up as a spine-tingling series."

He had no idea.

	1	2	3	4	
Cavaliers	24	12	27	17	=80
Bullets	24	22	17	16	=79

CLEVELAND

Player	FG-FGA	FT-FTA	Reb.	Ass.	Pts.
Brewer	1–3	1–4	7	3	3
Smith	7–17	3–4	5	4	17
Chones	5–18	2–3	7	1	12
Cleamons	6–18	2–2	5	1	14
Snyder	6–14	4–4	6	2	16
Thurmond	3–6	1–1	10	2	7
Carr	4–9	0–0	4	0	8
Russell	1–11	1–2	7	1	3
Walker	0–1	0–0	0	0	0
TOTAL	33–97	14–20	51	14	80

PORTLAND

Player	FG-FGA	FT-FTA	Reb.	Ass.	Pts.
Hayes	4–14	5–7	11	1	13
Robinson	6–15	3–5	13	0	15
Unseld	2–3	4–7	13	5	8
Bing	6–13	4–7	5	7	16
Chenier	8–22	3–4	5	0	19
Weatherspoon	2–8	2–2	4	1	6
Jones	0–1	2–2	1	0	2
Kozelko	0–0	0–0	0	0	0
Riordan	0–0	0–0	0	0	0
Haskins	0–0	0–0	0	0	0
TOTAL	28–76	23–34	52	14	79

Attendance: 17,988

CAVALIERS 124, LOS ANGELES LAKERS 120
MARCH 22, 1972

Footnote to History

In the early spring of 1972, the Los Angeles Lakers were desperately trying to rewrite history. Conversely, the Cavaliers, in their second year of existence, were just trying to create some history to call their own. These entirely different manifestos clashed on a Wednesday night at Cleveland Arena and would indeed provide historical significance for both franchises.

After more than a decade of near misses that included eight trips to the NBA Finals but no titles, the 1971–72 Lakers had a date with destiny. After a ho-hum 6–3 start to the season, Los Angeles ripped off a league record thirty-three straight victories, going more than two months without suffering a defeat. As the winter wore on, the Lakers were focused on breaking another record: most victories in a season. Five years before, the Philadelphia 76ers had gone 68–14, and as the final weeks of the 1971–72 season ticked away, the Lakers drew closer and closer to history.

They came to Cleveland on March 22 holding a 67–12 record, needing two victories in their final three games to set the mark. The Cavs, a woeful 22–56, had shown marginal improvement in their second year but were still a long way from competing with a team like Los Angeles. True enough, the Cavs had yet to beat the Lakers and twelve days earlier had been dusted in Los Angeles to the tune of a 132–98 drubbing. There was little reason to doubt the rematch would go any differently. Los Angeles, the top scoring team in the NBA, had future Hall-of-Famers Jerry West, Gail Goodrich, and Wilt Chamberlain. The Cavs would counter with unknowns Rick Roberson, John Johnson, and Bingo Smith.

Better than 10,000 fans—what would prove to be one of the largest crowds in Arena history—packed into the stands primarily to witness the Lakers tie the record. But the Cavaliers altered the script with a red-hot first quarter that saw them shoot 65 percent and sprint to a 40–25 lead. But L.A. turned the tables in the second quarter with a hot streak of its own and fought back to tie what was quickly becoming a wild contest.

All season long, the third quarter had been Cleveland's Achilles' heel, but this time, the Cavs actually built another lead, surging to an eleven-point advantage midway through the period. Naturally, however, the Lakers rebounded and tied the contest again early in the fourth. David was matching Goliath blow for blow. "I knew we had a chance when we didn't fold when they hit us with a hot streak in the third quarter," Bill Fitch would say later.

Everything was clicking. Roberson, a former Laker, had neutralized Chamberlain for most of the game, while scoring a career-high twenty-nine points. And Cleveland's top scorers weren't giving the Lakers any slack. Johnson hit for twenty-eight points, Smith for twenty-seven, and Butch Beard for twenty-four, matching West and Gail Goodrich, who each scored thirty-one. Despite Chamberlain's nineteen rebounds, Cleveland actually proved stronger than the Lakers on the boards, 51–48, led by Roberson's fourteen.

But it all appeared to go up in smoke when Roberson fouled out with a minute to play. What meager talent the Cavs had was almost solely limited to the starting lineup, and Cleveland had been burdened with a lack of depth all season. Once again, however, an unlikely result materialized. Walt Wesley came in off the bench to hit the game-clinching basket with fourteen seconds to play to secure a 124–120 victory, the biggest in the brief history of the Cavaliers. "We have the chance to say we beat the potential world champions tonight," Fitch said.

And beat them they had. The Lakers, who would go on to stomp the Knicks in the NBA Finals a month later, left the Arena impressed that night. For four quarters, the Cleveland Cavaliers were superior to the eventual world champs, and in the process had put a dent in the Lakers' historical quest. Los Angeles won its final two games to break the record with sixty-nine victories, but the Cavs had left their mark on the achievement with an immense upset that kept Los Angeles from reaching seventy wins—a barrier that would remain uncrossed for another quarter century.

There would be many victories over dominant teams in the years to come, but the '72 Lakers still stand as the finest team the Cavaliers have ever beaten—as well as the victims of perhaps the unlikeliest upset in franchise history.

	1	2	3	4	
Lakers	25	35	28	32	=120
Cavaliers	40	20	30	34	=124

LOS ANGELES

Player	FG	FT-FTA	Pts.
Chamberlain	10	3–9	23
Goodrich	11	9–12	31
Hairston	5	4–5	14
McMillian	6	0–0	12
Riley	2	0–0	4
Trapp	2	1–1	5
West	12	7–7	31
TOTAL	48	24–34	120

CLEVELAND

Player	FG	FT-FTA	Pts.
Beard	9	6–7	24
Carr	4	1–3	9
Johnson	8	12–12	28
Roberson	12	5–8	29
Smith	12	3–4	27
Sorenson	1	0–0	2
Washington	0	1–1	1
Wesley	2	0–0	4
TOTAL	48	28–35	124

Attendance: 10,819

#10

CAVALIERS 114, WASHINGTON WIZARDS 113 (OT)
MAY 5, 2006

Thirteen Years, Fourteen Seconds

In the thirteen years since the Cavaliers had won a playoff series, the Browns had ceased to exist and then been reborn, the once-forlorn Indians had captured six division titles and two pennants, and the structures all three teams played in had been destroyed and replaced.

And in that time, the Cavs had gone through eight head coaches and endured a stretch of six consecutive losing seasons. But there was something different about the team as it entered the 2006 playoffs. Not only had Cleveland simply qualified to the postseason for the first time in eight years—the longest drought in team history—but it won fifty games in the regular season for the first time since 1993. Most importantly, this would be LeBron James's first trip to the postseason—and Cleveland sports fans were as excited as a mother sending her firstborn off to kindergarten.

The third-year superstar had single-handedly rescued the Cavs from a sixty-five-loss debacle the year before he arrived, but a first-round best-of-seven series against Washington would be his first chance to truly prove his worth. He didn't disappoint, hitting the game-winning buckets in the final seconds of Games Three and Five and putting the Cavaliers in a position to end the series—and their thirteen-year drought—with a win at Washington's Verizon Center in Game Six.

But the Wizards, led by guard Gilbert Arenas, who had matched James almost point for point through the whole series, weren't going to make it easy. Washington sprinted to an early fourteen-point lead in the first quarter before Cleveland fought back to cut the margin to one at the half. The teams exchanged knockout punches in a classic second half before the Wizards grabbed a seven-point advantage with just over two minutes remaining. A three-pointer by Cleveland forward Donyell Marshall and a James basket narrowed the lead to 101–99, then with the clock ticking under thirty seconds, James made a key steal that resulted in guard Ronald Murray hitting two free throws to give Cleveland a one-point lead with 23.3 seconds to play.

After Arenas missed a driving layup that would have given Washington back the lead, the Cavs stretched the margin to three points and the Wizards had time for one final possession. As he had throughout the entire series, Arenas came through, nailing a thirty-foot jumper with 2.3 seconds left to tie the game. Once again, Cleveland and Washington would head to overtime in a series that was beginning to resemble their 1976 epic.

The nip-and-tuck battle continued through the extra session, but the Cavs appeared to run out of magic when Eric Snow threw the ball out of bounds with sixteen seconds left and Cleveland down one. Two seconds later, Arenas was sent to the line to try to make the lead a comfortable three points. But after coming through time and again, this time Arenas tanked, missing both free throws to give the Cavaliers new life—and set the stage for an unlikely hero.

Though he'd played in every regular season game, guard Damon Jones certainly wasn't one of the leaders of the team and in fact hadn't played at all in Game Six until coming in with fourteen seconds remaining in overtime. With all eyes in the arena focused on James, the Cavs prepared to cross up the Wizards. James took the inbound pass, but then split a double team and tossed the ball to Hughes, who rifled a pass to Jones along the baseline just inside the three-point arc. Jones fired up a shot which was perfect, giving the Cavs a 114–113 lead with 4.8 seconds left. Out of time-outs, the Wizards raced down the floor and Caron Butler missed an eighteen-foot jumper at the buzzer. The Cavaliers mobbed Jones at midcourt, celebrating their third one-point victory of the series. James had scored thirty-two points and Marshall had exploded for twenty-eight off the bench, but the star of the game was a guy who played fourteen seconds. "If he misses that shot," Marshall said of Jones's jumper, "we go to Game Seven, and you never know what would happen."

What did happen was a milestone achievement for LeBron James—the first of what fans hoped would be many playoff triumphs. "This is probably one of the best feelings I've had in a long time," James said. "It took me two years to get here and to finally be a part of it. I didn't want to just come in here and be happy just to be in the playoffs, but I wanted to try and win a playoff series, and we did a great job of doing that."

That they had. After a tense fifty-three minutes, an exciting six games, and thirteen excruciating years, the Cleveland Cavaliers had finally won a playoff series.

	1	2	3	4	OT	
Cavaliers	17	31	27	32	7	=114
Wizards	24	25	27	31	6	=113

CLEVELAND

Player	FG-FGA	FT-FTA	Reb.	Ass.	Pts.
James	15–25	1–3	7	7	32
Gooden	0–1	2–2	3	0	2
Ilgauskas	2–4	2–2	5	0	6
Hughes	3–17	2–2	3	12	9
Snow	2–8	4–4	4	1	8
Varejao	2–2	2–3	10	1	6
Marshall	11–15	2–4	8	1	28
Murray	7–12	6–6	4	2	21
Jones	1–1	0–0	0	0	2
TOTAL	43–85	21–26	44	24	114

3-Point Goals: 7–19 (Marshall 4–7, Murray 1–1, Hughes 1–4, James 1–6, Snow 0–1)

WASHINGTON

Player	FG-FGA	FT-FTA	Reb.	Ass.	Pts.
Butler	5–18	8–8	20	5	18
Jamison	6–17	2–2	4	5	15
Haywood	7–8	3–5	4	1	17
Jeffries	0–3	3–4	6	3	3
Arenas	14–27	4–8	5	11	36
Daniels	8–15	4–4	3	2	22
Ruffin	0–0	0–2	1	0	0
Thomas	1–2	0–0	2	0	2
TOTAL	41–90	24–33	45	27	113

3-Point Goals: 7–20 (Arenas 4–8, Daniels 2–4, Jamison 1–6, Butler 0–2)

Attendance: 20,173

A Banner Day

When Nick Mileti first conceived of the notion of a professional basketball team in Cleveland, he dreamed of this scenario—a huge crowd at a sparkling new arena cheering on a team playing for a championship.

On a crisp spring afternoon in 1976, his dream came true. It was the second-to-last game of what had become a remarkable season. After five years of painfully gradual progress, the Cavs had finally put it all together, fielding a team that was both talented and balanced, if not experienced. They'd clinched their first winning record in late March, then ten days later secured their first playoff berth. Now, with the New York Knicks in town for the home finale, the Cleveland Cavaliers had a chance to capture their first title.

Though it had seemed utterly preposterous early in the season, the Cavs had overthrown the defending Eastern Conference champion Washington Bullets—winners of the division five straight seasons—and now were on the brink of clinching the Central Division title. Perhaps just as historically significant, they also could secure home-court advantage for their upcoming playoff series with the Bullets. A win over the Knicks would clinch a tie, and if Washington were to lose to Boston the next day, Cleveland would win the title outright. With a crowd of better than 14,000 fans on hand and millions more tuned in to CBS's national broadcast, the Cavs announced loud and clear that they had arrived, regardless of what happened in Washington on Sunday.

The Knicks, out of the postseason picture for the first time in ten years, still hung tough. They grabbed a seven-point lead in the second quarter, and trailed by only three at the half. Then, after Cleveland surged to a fourteen-point lead, New York rallied to make a game of it in the fourth, closing the margin to 94–93 in the waning minutes.

But as they'd done all season, the Cavs responded when they had to. Austin Carr hit a crucial bucket on a drive, followed by key free throws by Bingo Smith and Campy Russell in the final minute to secure a 99–94 win. "It was a typical Cavalier victory," Jim Chones said. "Everyone contributed. It's been that way for the last season and a half."

As the Cavs and Knicks battled, twenty-five miles north the Indians held their home opener at Cleveland Stadium and, not surprisingly, lost to Detroit. The only bright spot of the day was when the final score of the Cavs' game flashed across the Stadium boards and the crowd paid tribute with a standing ovation. *Plain Dealer* sports editor Hal Lebovitz bemoaned his decision to head to the Stadium rather than the Coliseum: "I should have gone to see the Cavaliers, where my heart was."

Back in Richfield, hearts were pumping with devotion for the Cavs, who, as Bill Nichols wrote, finally had "established their credibility." By clinching a share of the division title, Nichols said, they'd "erased once and for all those dreadful memories of past years and those one-sided losses, wrong-way baskets, and sick jokes."

"It's been a long time coming," said a beaming Bingo Smith, the last of the original Cavs still on the roster, and anyone who'd witnessed the utter horror of the first season knew just how long it had been. Champagne was delivered to the Cleveland locker room, but Bill Fitch refused to allow it to be opened. "We've never celebrated a tie yet and that's what we have now," he said. "Bring it back in June and we'll drink it all."

The next day, the tie was broken when the Celtics knocked off the Bullets, 103–99. But the Saturday matinee triumph over New York before an adoring crowd and a rare national television audience would mark the moment in history in which the Cavaliers first became champions.

	1	2	3	4	
Knicks	23	25	22	24	=94
Cavaliers	22	29	33	15	=99

NEW YORK

Player	FG-FGA	FT-FTA	Reb.	Ass.	Pts.
Bradley	3–9	0–1	2	3	6
Haywood	8–25	2–2	18	2	18
Gianelli	3–8	0–0	4	2	6
Beard	2–7	1–2	4	4	5
Monroe	12–20	6–9	8	0	30
Barnett	5–10	2–3	1	3	12
Jackson	3–4	3–6	1	0	9
Walk	2–4	0–2	6	2	4
Davis	2–3	0–0	1	0	4
Wingo	0–0	0–0	0	0	0
TOTAL	40–90	14–25	45	16	94

CLEVELAND

Player	FG-FGA	FT-FTA	Reb.	Ass.	Pts.
Smith	6–13	3–4	2	1	15
Brewer	3–6	0–0	16	4	6
Chones	11–18	3–4	11	0	25
Snyder	2–8	2–2	3	1	6
Cleamons	5–17	3–4	6	7	13
Russell	7–12	9–11	5	0	23
Carr	5–13	0–0	3	1	10
Thurmond	0–1	0–0	3	1	0
Walker	0–3	1–2	0	1	1
TOTAL	39–91	21–27	49	16	99

Attendance: 14,326

#8

Instant Classic

Even in a town that had become accustomed to seeing huge crowds at sporting events subdued into an almost catatonic state of shock, the eerie silence of this Friday night throng was deafening.

Fans covered their faces with jittery hands. Small children stared at the arena floor in disbelief with tears beginning to well up behind stunned, glassy eyes. Once again, they'd allowed themselves to get their hopes up, contemplating visions of a championship parade in downtown Cleveland. And once again, it seemed, their hearts and dreams would be pulverized.

The contrast between this night and others in downtown Cleveland over the course of the previous winter was jarring. During the past seven months, every evening at Quicken Loans Arena had been a reason for celebration, an excuse to leave behind the disheartening news of the outside world—dominated by a miserable economy and the toll it was taking on what some claimed was a dying city. Against this backdrop, the Cavaliers had embarked on their finest season ever, winning a record sixty-six games and capturing the best won-loss mark in the NBA. Along the way, the Q had become basketball's proverbial lion's den, as the Cavs posted an astonishing 39–2 record on their home floor. And if anyone was going to knock the Cavs out of the playoffs, they'd have to do it by winning at least one game in Cleveland.

Now, with one second remaining in Game Two of the Eastern Conference finals, the suddenly red-hot Orlando Magic was on the brink of accomplishing the previously unthinkable. The Magic was one tick of the clock away from stealing back-to-back games in Cleveland and taking a choke hold on the best-of-seven series before it truly got started.

Many Cavalier fans were still trying to comprehend what had happened on this floor two nights before, when the home team somehow squandered a sixteen-point lead and lost by one on a three-point shot by Orlando in the waning seconds. Game Two followed a bizarrely similar script, with the Cavs dominating play early and cruising to a twenty-three-point advantage. However, behind uncanny long-distance shooting accuracy, the Magic gradually chipped away at the lead and transformed the fourth quarter into something akin to a heavyweight title bout.

Though Cleveland led by nine with nine minutes to play, Orlando caught fire once again. When guard Courtney Lee hit a running jumper with 5:27 remaining to give the Magic its first lead at 86–84, the here-we-go-again groans could be heard all over northeast Ohio. The teams traded punches throughout the final minutes until the Cavaliers appeared to construct a slight cushion when they sneaked to a three-point lead with less than a minute left. A stop away from assuming control, the Cavs' defense was unable to prevent Orlando forward Hedo Turkoglu from drilling a game-tying three-pointer with forty-eight seconds left. Cleveland's following possession ended when LeBron James was whistled for traveling on a drive to the basket, then Orlando caught another break when Cavs' guard Sasha Pavlovic was called for a foul with 13.3 seconds left that allowed the Magic to further milk the clock and set up a final shot.

And as it had done all night, the Magic responded. Again it was Turkoglu, penetrating to the foul line and tossing up a soft jumper over Pavlovic, which stroked through the net to give Orlando a 95–93 lead with exactly one second remaining.

Not surprisingly, despite the arena staff's attempt to get the crowd excited during the ensuing time-out, the fans were hushed, drained, and down. Their only hope was a miracle. But even in the depths of their despair, they knew there was a man on the floor capable of delivering one.

Named the NBA's Most Valuable Player three weeks before, LeBron James was already having a marvelous series. He'd exploded for a career-playoff-high forty-nine points in Game One and had already accounted for thirty-two more in the second game to go along with four rebounds and five assists. And he knew he was capable of getting off a good shot in the time allowed. "A second is a long time for me," he would say later. "As a kid you practice those moments." The problem was that everyone in the building—including the Orlando Magic—knew he wanted the ball.

Appropriately, James was matched with Turkoglu, who stood two inches taller. As Cleveland point guard Mo Williams took the ball from the official along the sideline near midcourt, James cut toward the basket from the free-throw line, then quickly jerked back outside, creating a fraction of separation between him and Turkoglu. It was all he needed. "I was going to come get the ball no matter what happened," James said.

He caught Williams's inbound pass at the top of the key beyond the three-point arc, instantly squared his body to the basket, and launched a twenty-five-foot shot. "Honest answer," James would say, "when I caught it square, it felt great. It wasn't like a desperation shot."

As the final buzzer echoed, the ball spun through the tension-crackling air of the arena with picture-perfect rotation and rattled through the cylinder. It was, as Orlando center Dwight Howard would describe later, like a scene from a movie.

The Q's pensive silence broke in an eruption of relief and joy from 20,562 emotionally drained fans—ten times louder than the biggest roar he'd ever heard in the building before, James said later. He sprinted back toward the Cleveland bench, where he was mobbed by his teammates. Watching from the sideline where he'd made the inbound pass, Williams gently raised his hands to his head and bowed down almost as if in prayer.

Players, fans, coaches, broadcasters, and writers alike knew they'd just witnessed a defining moment in basketball history. TNT analyst Ernie Johnson appropriately called it "one for the ages." Cleveland coach Mike Brown, who'd ladled out more than his share of LeBron superlatives in the previous four seasons, described it simply as an "amazing shot by an amazing player."

"Biggest shot I've made in my career," James said. "That's a shot you will see for a long time, you know?"

The shot quickly was compared to other dramatic buzzer-beaters in NBA history. And of course, in Cleveland, it was held up against *The* Shot—Michael Jordan's series-clinching jumper that eliminated a marvelous Cavs team twenty years before. But the swift verdict came back that James's shot was not only more meaningful because it came later in the postseason, but that it was also much more technically impressive: with one second in which to work instead of three, from eight feet farther out, and with a taller defender in his face.

Even Turkoglu was impressed. "He just made a crazy shot," he sighed. "You can't do anything about that."

"That was a pretty good game, what do y'all think?" Williams asked reporters afterward. "The basketball gods love us. That was an instant classic."

In that instant, LeBron James had turned disaster into triumph. And though Orlando would go on to defeat the Cavaliers in the series, James's miraculous shot would become the lasting image of the entire record-breaking season.

And emblematic of the heroics of the greatest player in Cavalier history.

	1	2	3	4	
Magic	16	28	25	26	=95
Cavaliers	30	26	19	21	=96

ORLANDO

Player	FG-FGA	FT-FTA	Reb.	Ass.	Pts.
Lewis	6–15	7–9	5	1	23
Turkoglu	9–17	1–2	2	4	21
Howard	3–8	4–8	18	4	10
Alston	1–7	2–2	1	2	4
Lee	4–9	2–2	0	1	11
Pietrus	4–5	0–0	1	0	10
Johnson	2–4	1–2	0	4	5
Gortat	2–2	0–0	3	0	4
Redick	3–4	0–0	0	0	7
Battie	0–0	0–0	0·	0	0
TOTAL	34–71	17–25	30	16	95

3-Point Goals: 10–23 (Lewis 4–7, Turkoglu 2–4, Alston 0–3, Lee 1–3, Pietrus 2–3, Johnson 0–1, Redick 1–2)

CLEVELAND

Player	FG-FGA	FT-FTA	Reb.	Ass.	Pts.
Varejao	2–5	0–1	4	1	4
James	12–23	10–12	4	5	35
Ilgauskas	5–13	2–2	15	2	12
Williams	7–21	4–5	5	5	19
West	4–7	3–3	5	1	12
Pavlovic	4–7	0–1	1	2	9
Wallace	0–0	0–0	2	1	0
Smith	1–1	2–2	2	0	5
Gibson	0–0	0–0	0	0	0
Kinsey	0–0	0–0	0	0	0
TOTAL	35–77	21–26	38	17	96

3-Point Goals: 5–19 (James 1–3, Ilgauskas 0–2, Williams 1–6, West 1–4, Pavlovic 1–3, Smith 1–1)

Attendance: 20,562

CAVALIERS 107, CHICAGO BULLS 81
MAY 21, 1992

Revenge of the Marshmallow Men

While the Cavaliers and Boston Celtics were engaged in a crisp, classy playoff series that better resembled a chess match, in the other 1992 Eastern Conference semifinal, the Chicago Bulls and New York Knicks were role-playing a military junta. Throughout a seven-game series brimming with apelike machismo, the Bulls and Knicks literally beat one another senseless, trading punches, cheap shots, and body blows. The Bulls emerged bloody but unbowed and saw the well-mannered Cavaliers as a two-week vacation. "It's just a whole different atmosphere," Michael Jordan said. "You don't have to worry about going to the basket and getting creamed. The doctors aren't sitting there nervous about having to treat everybody."

Though comments such as these might have upset the Cavs, the team did little to counter the contention in Game One. Chicago steamrolled past Cleveland, 103–89, and commentators and writers from coast to coast only expected more of the same. "If the Knicks arrived from a back alley," Jay Mariotti wrote in the *Chicago Sun-Times,* "the Cavs came straight from the public library . . . Everyone wanted a restoration of clean play, but who asked for a church recital?" The *Chicago Tribune's* Melissa Isaacson likened the Cavs to the Hardy Boys, and Chicago forward Horace Grant opined, "This is the type of series people can bring their kids to."

While some of the criticism was well founded and appropriate, it quickly took a malicious turn. Reporters began referring to the Cavaliers as "marshmallows" and "cream puffs," predicting they were too nice to compete for a championship. "There is a sense," Bud Shaw wrote in the *Plain Dealer,* "that there might as well be five cardboard cutouts of Cavs players on the court in this series." Even normally reserved Cavs' GM Wayne Embry was steaming. "It bothers the hell out of me," he said. "I hope it bothers the players. I wouldn't want anybody calling me a marshmallow."

The Chicago media and the Bulls themselves were already looking toward the NBA Finals, now just three more cakewalk victories away. But in Game Two, the Cavaliers heated up like marshmallows over a campfire and blew the Bulls into Lake Michigan.

It was clear in the opening minutes these were not the cream puff Cavaliers who had gone through the motions in the first game. Jordan was stripped the first two times he touched the ball, and the Cavs' defense threw the Chicago attack into reverse. The Bulls missed their first thirteen shots as Cleveland rolled to first-half leads of 15–3, 28–9, and 46–19. Jordan, who had used the Cavaliers as a springboard to superstardom, missed nine of his first ten shots and would score just twenty for the night while committing six turnovers.

The margin was twenty-six at the half after the Cavs shot an amazing 68 percent from the floor, sparked by twenty-one points from Mark Price, who drilled four of five three-pointers. The sellout crowd booed the defending world champions off the floor. Things became surreal in the second half when the lead swelled to thirty-five. "At times I looked up at the scoreboard and I couldn't believe what I was seeing," Brad Daugherty said. And he wasn't the only one. The cadre of writers who had questioned the Cavaliers' manhood was now looking for cover. "All those people who wrote us off can write something else," Price said afterward. "They can go drive in the lake. They can eat crow."

The final was an astonishing 107–81—the worst Chicago defeat in nearly three years and the largest postseason margin of victory in Cavalier history. There would be no more doubting the Cavaliers' talent or manhood. They'd put a spanking on Jordan and the Bulls that would forever echo through the corridors of both franchises.

Interestingly, the emblematic image of the blowout came prior to Game Three at Richfield Coliseum when a clip from the film *Ghostbusters* played on the telescreens, showing a gigantic Stay Puft Marshmallow Man stomping through New York City to the roaring delight of a capacity crowd.

On that Thursday night in the Windy City, the Bulls discovered the Cavs may not have had the thuglike mentality of the Knicks, but they could play basketball. And everyone discovered how tough a marshmallow could be.

	1	2	3	4	
Cavaliers	30	29	18	30	=107
Bulls	14	19	17	31	=81

CLEVELAND

Player	FG-FGA	FT-FTA	Reb.	Ass.	Pts.
Nance	5–8	4–4	4	1	14
Sanders	3–5	0–0	4	1	6
Daugherty	11–20	6–7	9	4	28
Ehlo	3–7	0–0	4	7	6
Price	5–9	9–9	5	7	23
Williams	5–9	0–0	6	2	10
Brandon	1–4	0–0	3	2	2
Ferry	2–2	0–0	5	0	4
Battle	3–7	2–2	1	2	8
James	1–4	2–4	1	0	4
Kerr	0–2	0–0	0	0	0
Phills	0–2	2–2	2	0	2
TOTAL	39–79	25–28	44	26	107

3-Point Goals: 4–7 (Price 4–5, Ehlo 0–1, Kerr 0–1)

CHICAGO

Player	FG-FGA	FT-FTA	Reb.	Ass.	Pts.
Pippen	4–14	3–6	9	3	11
Grant	5–10	0–0	12	0	10
Cartwright	0–4	0–0	0	0	0
Paxson	2–6	0–0	0	0	5
Jordan	7–22	6–7	11	3	20
King	5–10	3–6	2	2	13
Armstrong	7–10	2–3	3	2	16
Levingston	0–1	0–0	3	1	0
Hodges	0–5	0–0	1	0	0
S. Williams	0–2	0–0	2	0	0
Perdue	1–2	0–0	3	3	2
Hansen	2–3	0–1	2	3	4
TOTAL	33–89	14–23	48	17	81

3-Point Goals: 1–7 (Paxson 1–2, Hansen 0–1, Pippen 0–2, Hodges 0–2)

Attendance: 18,676

#6

CAVALIERS 154, LOS ANGELES LAKERS 153 (4 OT)
JANUARY 29, 1980

Beyond the Point of Exhaustion

When the evening began, there was absolutely nothing special about it. By the time it was over, it would stand as one of the most memorable dates in the history of professional basketball.

The Cavaliers' late 1970s slump had carried over to the new decade, and as the first month of 1980 came to a close, Cleveland was out of playoff contention with a 22–31 record. But with the resurgent Los Angeles Lakers in town, a surprisingly big crowd for a Tuesday night was expected at the Coliseum. Led by rookie phenom Magic Johnson and venerable center Kareem Abdul-Jabbar, Los Angeles was about to begin a wildly successful string that would see the team capture nine conference titles in twelve years. They'd handled the Cavs by fourteen points in their first meeting two months earlier, and with Cleveland's second-leading scorer, Campy Russell, out with an injury, and Jim Chones, the most dominant player in Cavs' history, now playing for Los Angeles, there was little doubt the Lakers would complete the season sweep.

The Cavaliers started fast, grabbing an eleven-point halftime lead, but L.A. caught fire in the third quarter and took a lead into the fourth. Then it was Cleveland's turn to rally with a remarkable run down the stretch capped by a jump shot by forward Mike Mitchell to tie the contest at 114 with twenty-nine seconds left. Regulation ended with the score still knotted and the teams plunged into overtime—neither knowing their night was just beginning.

The Cavs snuck to a 126–122 lead with nineteen seconds remaining, but Los Angeles guard Norm Nixon hit a jumper, and then forward Michael Cooper stole a pass and connected on a ten-footer to tie the score with seven seconds left. Cleveland failed to score on its final possession and the teams tumbled into a second overtime. Then a third. Then a fourth. Both teams persevered through countless momentum swings and onsetting exhaustion, but finally, in the opening seconds of the fourth overtime, the Lakers appeared to catch the tide-turning break. Cleveland center Dave Robisch, who was having a wonderful game, fouled out, leaving little-used substitute Bill Willoughby as the only option left to guard the seven-foot-four Abdul-Jabbar. And though Kareem was having a marvelous game of his own—winding up with forty-two points, seventeen rebounds, and eight blocks—Willoughby rose to the occasion and forever etched his name in Cavalier lore.

Still, Los Angeles slid into the driver's seat when forward Jamaal Wilkes nailed a fifteen-foot jumper to put the Lakers up 151–146 with 1:47 remaining. Running solely on fumes and motivated by nothing more than pride, the Cavs once again battled back. Mitchell connected from twelve feet, then Willoughby scored over Abdul-Jabbar to pull the home team within a single point. With eighteen seconds remaining, Abdul-Jabbar fouled out, and Willoughby hit the ensuing free throws to give the Cavs the lead. On the following possession, Nixon drove into the lane and fired up a shot that Willoughby blocked with five seconds left, but Willoughby was whistled for goaltending. The crowd booed wildly as replays were shown on the telescreens, realizing the Cavs now needed to score in the final five seconds or suffer a heartbreaking defeat in what had somehow become an epic contest.

Foots Walker inbounded to Mitchell, who drove the lane hard only to be fouled by Chones with two seconds left. Chones became the sixth player to foul out on the night and Mitchell, playing his fifty-ninth minute, headed to the line with a chance to end the marathon. "Just to stop this game," he said, "I knew I had to make both free throws."

And make them he did, his thirty-third and thirty-fourth points of the game. And after a last-second desperation heave by Los Angeles missed, at 11:20 P.M., the longest game in Cavalier history came to a close three hours and seventeen minutes after it began: a legendary 154–153 four-overtime triumph. "You don't unwind after something like this," said Cleveland guard Randy Smith. "It was a great game—a classic game."

One that lives on in the team's media guide to this day. Ten Cleveland records were broken and still stand. Meanwhile, the Lakers set the league mark for most points ever scored by a losing team. "I don't know if this was the best game I've ever been in," Robisch said, "but as far as excitement and thrills go, it definitely was the best game." A pedestrian January contest had taken on the flavor of a grueling heavyweight title bout. "Their chances of making the playoffs now are slim," Nichols wrote, "but they played Tuesday as though the championship were at stake."

Though the Cavs had been "down to the count of nine more times than a wobbly heavyweight," as Nichols wrote, they fought on despite not having any tangible motivation. It was a detail Hal Lebovitz noted, appreciating "the human drama of men playing beyond the point of exhaustion in a game that had no special significance expect for that inner ingredient that makes an athlete excel—competitive pride."

In the history of the Cleveland Cavaliers, there was never a night that contained more of that pride.

	1	2	3	4	OT1	OT2	OT3	OT4	
Lakers	24	23	36	31	12	10	8	9	=153
Cavaliers	30	28	22	34	12	10	8	10	=154

LOS ANGELES

Player	FG-FGA	FT-FTA	Reb.	Pts.
Wilkes	10–22	3–3	14	23
Chones	5–11	2–4	14	12
Abdul-Jabbar	18–35	6–8	17	42
Nixon	9–19	2–2	1	20
Johnson	12–18	6–7	11	30
Haywood	4–8	6–6	8	14
Cooper	5–8	2–2	1	12
Byrnes	0–1	0–0	0	0
Mack	0–0	0–0	0	0
TOTAL	63–122	27–32	66	153

CLEVELAND

Player	FG-FGA	FT-FTA	Reb.	Pts.
Mitchell	14–22	6–6	9	34
Willoughby	6–12	4–5	10	16
Robisch	14–26	4–5	10	32
R. Smith	13–35	5–8	5	31
Walker	4–7	0–0	7	8
K. Carr	9–16	5–8	12	23
W. Smith	1–8	0–0	2	2
Lambert	4–8	0–0	5	8
A. Carr	0–8	0–0	1	0
TOTAL	65–142	24–32	61	154

Attendance: 13,820

CAVALIERS 109, DETROIT PISTONS 107 (2 OT)
MAY 31, 2007

Like in a Video Game

If the Cavs were going to surprise the world and secure their first trip to the NBA Finals, they would have to defeat the Detroit Pistons on their home court—something that hadn't happened much in recent history.

A heavy underdog going into the 2007 Eastern Conference finals in which Detroit held the home-court advantage, Cleveland had let two golden opportunities for a win at The Palace of Auburn Hills slip away, losing heartbreakers in Games One and Two by the identical scores of 79–76. The loss in the first game garnered the most discussion when, trailing by two in the waning seconds, LeBron James passed up a potential game-tying shot attempt when he saw Donyell Marshall had a wide-open look beyond the three-point line. Marshall's shot missed and the Pistons got the rebound, leading many in the national media to question not only whether James should have taken the shot himself but also whether he actually wanted the ball in that kind of pressure situation against a strong defense. A week later, that notion would sound utterly ridiculous.

Down two games to none, the Cavs rallied to take Games Three and Four at Quicken Loans Arena, then returned to the Palace for a Thursday night clash in Game Five, in which the victor would find itself one win away from the Finals. The tone for what would become an unforgettable night was set in the opening minutes when Detroit forward Antonio McDyess clothes-lined Cleveland's Anderson Varejao on a drive to the basket, and James confronted the Piston star. McDyess was ejected, James was given a technical foul, and for the remainder of the night, the hostile Detroit crowd booed the Cavs' star every time he touched the ball.

Between the crowd and the Pistons' commitment to stopping him, James was held to a relatively harmless nineteen points midway through the fourth quarter.

Then, as if seeing the Cavs' wonderful season beginning to evaporate before him, the mighty James very quietly began to take over the game, encapsulating a comment he'd made earlier in the series: "I live for the fourth quarter."

After James hit a huge three-point shot with 2:15 left to cut a four-point Detroit lead to one, the Cavs crept to a one-point advantage in the final minute. Detroit's Chauncey Billups then drilled a three-pointer with twenty-three seconds left to put the Pistons up two, but James responded with a powerful drive and dunk to tie the game at ninety-one with 9.5 seconds remaining. The Cavs and Pistons went to overtime, and LeBron only got better.

Despite being double- and triple-teamed, James continued to score. He'd blow past five defenders for a dunk and then hit a jump shot with a Piston in his face. The Cavs took a 100–96 lead with thirty-three seconds left after a James' twenty-foot jumper with one second on the shot clock. They appeared to be in the driver's seat, but Detroit rallied. Billups was fouled by guard Eric Snow with 3.1 seconds left, and he calmly swished two free throws to tie the contest and force a second overtime.

This time, it was Detroit that pulled ahead, taking a 107–104 lead with under two minutes to play. But as he'd done all night, James came through when needed. This time, he hit perhaps the most incredible shot in Cavalier history—driving to his left and double-teamed twenty-five feet from the basket—James stopped and launched a fadeaway three-pointer that exploded through the cylinder to tie the contest with 1:14 remaining. It was a shot, as Joe Tait told his radio audience, that people in Cleveland would be talking about for a month.

A minute later, still tied at 107, the Cavs had the ball with the clock winding down under ten seconds. Though every person in the Western Hemisphere knew LeBron would wind up taking the Cavs' final shot, the Pistons were helpless to stop him. Starting a drive forty feet from the basket, James blew through the lane past the entire Detroit defense for an uncontested layup to put the Cavs up with 2.2 seconds left. When Billups's running fourteen-footer at the buzzer rimmed out, the Cavaliers had captured perhaps the most impressive postseason victory in team history. But its significance was overshadowed by the incredible individual performance turned in by LeBron James.

In fifty minutes of play, James scored forty-eight points, ripped down nine rebounds, and dished out seven assists. But perhaps most important was when the majority of his points were scored. James notched Cleveland's final seven points of the fourth quarter and then scored every single point of the two overtime sessions. Altogether, LeBron scored Cleveland's final twenty-five points and twenty-nine of its last thirty. It was instantly revered as one of the greatest postseason performances in NBA history. "This was the single best game I've ever seen on this level and in this atmosphere, hands down," said Cavs' coach Mike Brown. "He was absolutely phenomenal."

"Some of the things he does are like in a video game," Cleveland forward Scot Pollard said. "You think, 'You can't do that in real life.' I've seen a lot of great performances and guys score over fifty, but not in a pressure situation like tonight in a game that means so much to an organization."

James was understandably weary afterward. "I feel tired," he said. "I feel beat up. I feel fatigued. None of this would have mattered if we had lost."

But they had won, and it certainly did matter—thanks to a performance that instantly engraved itself in the portrait of professional basketball.

	1	2	3	4	OT	OT2	
Cavaliers	23	28	19	21	9	9	=109
Pistons	29	23	18	21	9	7	=107

CLEVELAND

Player	FG-FGA	FT-FTA	Reb.	Ass.	Pts.
James	18–33	10–14	9	7	48
Gooden	3–10	1–2	6	1	7
Ilgauskas	6–9	4–6	8	2	16
Pavlovic	2–10	1–2	9	1	6
Hughes	2–3	3–5	1	1	9
Varejao	3–6	3–4	3	0	9
Marshall	0–1	0–0	3	0	0
Gibson	2–7	6–6	0	1	11
Da. Jones	1–2	0–0	0	0	3
Snow	0–1	0–0	0	0	0
Pollard	0–0	0–0	0	0	0
TOTAL	37–82	28–39	39	13	109

3-Point Goals: 7–15 (Hughes 2–2, James 2–3, Da. Jones 1–2, Pavlovic 1–3, Gibson 1–3, Marshall 0–1, Snow 0–1)

DETROIT

Player	FG-FGA	FT-FTA	Reb.	Ass.	Pts.
Prince	4–13	1–2	9	3	10
Wallace	4–13	9–10	8	2	17
Webber	9–13	2–4	7	0	20
Hamilton	7–18	12–12	2	5	26
Billups	6–13	6–9	7	4	21
McDyess	1–2	0–0	1	0	2
Maxiell	2–2	5–6	5	0	9
Hunter	1–5	0–0	4	2	2
Delfino	0–1	0–0	0	2	0
Davis	0–0	0–0	2	0	0
TOTAL	34–80	35–43	45	18	107

3-Point Goals: 4–14 (Billups 3–7, Prince 1–2, Delfino 0–1, Hamilton 0–1, Hunter 0–1, Wallace 0–2)

Attendance: 22,076

A Religious Experience

"Those [expletive deleted]s won't win another game."

The words flowed like water out of the mouth of Washington Bullets' owner Abe Pollin after his team had outhustled and outplayed the Cleveland Cavaliers in Game Four of their 1976 Eastern Conference semifinal. With the best-of-seven series now knotted at two games apiece, Washington once again had the momentum, and if the Bullets could pick up another win in Richfield as they had in Game One, they would move a step closer to a second straight conference title, while the Cavs would find themselves one loss from elimination.

But Washington would now also have to contend with the tidal wave of public support that the Cavaliers found themselves surfing on. Thanks to the magic of television, basketball fans across the country were witnessing one of the great coming-of-age stories in NBA history, as the Cavs had transformed from laughingstock to championship contender. More than 21,000 would pack into the Coliseum on a Thursday night to see if the belles of the ball could keep the dance going.

Early on, it appeared the Cavs would coast. They took a ten-point lead into the second quarter and led by nine at the half. But, almost as if on cue, the seasoned Bullets fought back, and Dan Coughlin described the fourth quarter as "a struggle of two great rivers—the Amazon and the Mississippi—battling for territorial rights and washing back and forth across each other."

With the crowd roaring on each possession, the fateful final minute began with Dick Snyder connecting from twenty-five feet to give the Cavs a 90–89 lead. Then Phil Chenier responded for Washington, hitting a short baseline shot to give the Bullets back the lead. "From then on," Bill Nichols wrote, "it was pure science fiction."

On Cleveland's ensuing possession, Washington's Elvin Hayes stole a pass with just over ten seconds left, and the Cavs were forced to foul to stop the clock. Campy Russell hooked Hayes, sending the star forward to the line with seven seconds remaining for two shots which—in the era before the three-point shot—could ice the game. Yet somehow Hayes, who had made nine of his previous twelve foul shots, missed them both. Jim Brewer grabbed the rebound and the Cavs took time with six seconds left.

After a Washington foul on the first inbound attempt, Snyder passed the ball in to Bingo Smith coming off a screen by Jim Chones. Smith, mirroring his game-winning heroics in the waning seconds of Game Two, dribbled twice and launched a running twenty-foot shot. As it left his fingers, he knew it would fall short. "At first I thought the ball would hit the front of the rim and come back to me," Smith said. "Then I saw it was short and I was hoping somebody would get it."

Somebody did. Cavs' guard Jim Cleamons could also tell by the flight of the basketball that it wasn't going in, and he instantly charged beneath the basket to await the opportunity to grab the rebound. "Very few men on the floor were thinking like Clem," Snyder said. "Clem was the only one moving for the ball." The ball fell short of the rim and landed in Cleamons's hands. In one fluid motion, he flipped the ball back up toward the hoop.

It rolled around the cylinder and, as the buzzer sounded, hung motionless on the left side. The crowd stood breathless on its feet for a perfect, frozen moment.

Then the ball fell through the hoop, and the silence erupted in a cacophony of jubilation. For the second time in a week, the Cavs had defeated the Washington Bullets and the final buzzer with a miraculous score. "I couldn't believe it," Chones said. "We did it twice . . . This shot and Bingo's last week were the two greatest shots I ever saw." Sullen Bullets' center Wes Unseld echoed the sentiment: "I never saw it happen like this twice in one series."

As a result, the magical Cavaliers now led the series three games to two and were just one victory away from their first-ever playoff triumph. The stars had aligned for this once-haunted franchise, epitomized by Cleamons's unorthodox tip-in. "It just happened," he said with a shrug. "I was going to the offensive board and was fortunate to be in the right place at the right time."

Not unlike Cleveland sports fans, who had fallen in love with their basketball team. "Cavalier basketball is becoming a religious experience," Coughlin wrote, "breaking attendance records each time the Cavs take the floor. They can stop counting the crowd by heads. They should measure it in decibels."

Or in miracles.

	1	2	3	4	
Bullets	23	26	22	20	=91
Cavaliers	33	25	18	16	=92

WASHINGTON

Player	FG-FGA	FT-FTA	Reb.	Ass.	Pts.
Hayes	8–15	9–14	13	1	25
Weatherspoon	5–14	1–2	11	1	11
Unseld	2–4	2–2	6	2	6
Bing	6–14	6–8	2	6	18
Chenier	7–16	3–3	1	1	17
Haskins	0–3	0–2	0	0	0
Jones	3–7	6–8	4	1	12
Robinson	1–2	0–0	3	0	2
Riordan	0–0	0–0	0	0	0
TOTAL	32–75	27–39	40	12	91

CLEVELAND

Player	FG-FGA	FT-FTA	Reb.	Ass.	Pts.
Smith	7–16	1–2	4	3	15
Brewer	4–13	5–6	12	3	13
Chones	4–14	4–4	8	0	12
Snyder	12–18	2–2	2	4	26
Cleamons	2–9	2–2	9	4	6
Carr	1–4	0–2	1	3	2
Russell	6–13	6–7	6	1	18
Thurmond	0–2	0–0	7	0	0
Walker	0–0	0–0	0	0	0
TOTAL	36–89	20–25	49	18	92

Attendance: 21,312

CAVALIERS 122, BOSTON CELTICS 104
MAY 17, 1992

Seventh Heaven

It was like a sixteen-year-old kid taking on his dad in the driveway for the keys to the car that Saturday night.

On a bright, breezy Sunday afternoon in May, the Cavaliers faced one of the defining moments in their history. For just the second time ever, Cleveland would play in a Game Seven, hosting the Boston Celtics in a winner-take-all duel to conclude a back-and-forth Eastern Conference semifinal series.

While the Cavs were rewriting their own history, the Boston Celtics had essentially been born in the middle of a Game Seven. In their rich history, they'd played in twenty-seven, winning an astonishing seventeen. Since the triumphant trio of Larry Bird, Robert Parish, and Kevin McHale had joined forces more than ten years before, the Celts had played in ten deciding playoff games. It was a magical era on the brink of coming to an end, as age and injuries had pushed Bird to the conclusion of a legendary career. Over that same period, Cleveland reached the deciding game of a playoff series three times and was defeated in all three. "It's Game Seven with Boston," Bud Shaw wrote in the *Plain Dealer.* "A wonderful opportunity? Yes. A horrifying concept? Oh, yes. The sky is beautifully blue and falling."

While Cavs fans may have been nervous, they were still optimistic. When the Coliseum box office opened Saturday morning—less than twelve hours after Cleveland suffered a thirty-one-point loss in Boston that forced the seventh game—500 fans were already in line waiting to purchase tickets. The 7,000 tickets that remained were snatched up in two hours.

Long before the 2 P.M. tip-off on Sunday, the Coliseum was packed and roaring, evoking memories of Cleveland's other Game Seven sixteen years before. Fans checked their nervousness and anxiety at the door, symbolized by a six-by-eight-foot cardboard sign propped up in front of the Coliseum exit on Boston Mills Road reading "Larry Bird's Last Game Next Right."

To everyone's surprise, the game unfolded like a storybook for the Cavs and a wide-awake nightmare for the seasoned Celtics. On Boston's first possession, Parish dribbled the ball off his foot and Craig Ehlo scooped it up and took it the length of the floor for a layup. A tidal wave of ovation crashed down onto the floor, and the Cavs were off and running. Sparked by a smothering defense while hitting eight of their first ten shots, they sprinted to leads of 13–2 and 19–8. "The idea was to go out early and keep attacking, attacking, attacking," Brad Daugherty would say. Suddenly, a Boston team that had been sharp and effective throughout the playoffs looked like a collection of half-court, over-forty church league players. "They took us out of everything we wanted to do," Bird said. Putting on a passing clinic, the Cavs shot an amazing 73 percent in the first quarter as they took a 35–21 lead, led by sixteen points from Daugherty and nine points and four assists from Mark Price, who continually sliced through the Boston defense. And things would only get better.

Boston forward Reggie Lewis, who had been a thorn in the Cavs' side all series long, didn't hit a basket until midway through the second quarter. When Cleveland's iron grip on the contest loosened a little just before halftime, allowing the Celtics to cut the deficit to ten, Cavs' forward Mike Sanders sparked a 10–2 run to close the half with Cleveland up 65–47.

Just before the Cavs returned to the floor after intermission, team leaders Daugherty and Price called the team together in the locker room and pointed out that they had a chance to accomplish something very special. With the Cavs playing possibly the best single game in team history and the crowd rocking, the second half played out like the last day of school. The lead swelled to twenty-seven, and by the fourth quarter, the focus had turned to Cleveland's second-ever trip to the Eastern Conference finals. The final was 122–104, what McHale called the most painful loss he'd ever suffered. "When the flood gates open like that," he said, "the water just keeps pouring through." The Cavs had replaced the Celtics as the league's personification of fundamentally sound basketball, and both sides knew it. "We lost to a great team," Boston coach Chris Ford said. "We gave them the best we had."

"They taught us a lot in this series," Sanders said. "They taught us how to play like champions." And play like champions they had. They shot 59 percent from the floor and 84 percent from the free-throw line. Six Cavaliers scored in double figures as the unselfishness became contagious. Cleveland collected an astonishing forty-two assists on its forty-nine baskets, while outrebounding Boston 45–31 and outscoring them 46–22 in the paint and 35–12 in fast break points. Reflecting that dominance, Daugherty outscored Parish, 27–2, and outrebounded him, 9–3. And after Bird was limited to twelve points in thirty-three minutes, thanks to a smothering defensive performance by Sanders, the sign on Boston Mills Road turned out to be prophetic. The Richfield Coliseum had indeed been the site of Larry Bird's final professional basketball game.

But more importantly, it had been the setting for one of the most glorious moments in Cavalier history.

"It was, in all senses, a community effort," Bill Livingston wrote in the *Plain Dealer,* "every player just at the zenith of his game, every fan swept up in the cascade of sensational basketball, the whole place thundering with the sweet release of years of frustration, all the what-ifs and could've-beens, all the baggage of the past, all thrown exultantly aside in one joyous afternoon."

	1	2	3	4	
Celtics	21	26	24	33	=104
Cavaliers	35	30	30	27	=122

BOSTON

Player	FG-FGA	FT-FTA	Reb.	Ass.	Pts.
Bird	6–9	0–0	5	4	12
Gamble	2–11	2–2	2	3	6
Parish	1–2	0–0	3	0	2
Lewis	9–18	4–6	3	3	22
Bagley	4–6	1–1	0	5	9
Brown	7–11	4–6	2	5	18
McHale	6–14	3–4	5	0	15
Pinckney	5–9	2–3	9	0	12
Kleine	0–3	0–0	2	0	0
Fox	3–3	0–0	0	0	8
TOTAL	43–86	16–22	31	20	104

3-Point Goals: 2–6 (Fox 2–2, Lewis 0–1, McHale 0–1, Brown 0–2)

CLEVELAND

Player	FG-FGA	FT-FTA	Reb.	Ass.	Pts.
Nance	7–14	1–2	9	8	15
Sanders	6–11	5–6	6	2	17
Daugherty	9–11	9–11	9	6	27
Ehlo	5–7	0–0	4	6	12
Price	7–15	0–0	5	8	15
Williams	7–10	6–6	8	1	20
Brandon	3–6	0–0	2	6	6
Kerr	1–4	0–0	0	2	2
Battle	1–3	0–0	1	0	2
Ferry	2–2	0–0	0	0	4
James	0–2	0–0	0	1	0
Phills	1–1	0–0	1	2	2
TOTAL	49–86	21–25	45	42	122

3-Point Goals: 3–10 (Ehlo 2–4, Price 1–4, Brandon 0–2)

Attendance: 20,273

CAVALIERS 98, DETROIT PISTONS 82
JUNE 2, 2007

Lit Up Like Las Vegas

The Cleveland Cavaliers had never been so close to their dreams.

After a stunning, dramatic victory in Game Five of the Eastern Conference finals two nights before, the Cavs were one win away from the NBA Finals for the first time in their history. With a triumph over the Detroit Pistons before an adoring crowd at Quicken Loans Arena, Cleveland's reputation as a long-suffering sports city would soften just a bit. However, with a Cavs' loss, followed by a Game Seven defeat in Michigan, the albatross of heartbreak would tighten like a noose around Cleveland's neck.

That's precisely what had happened one year earlier when the Cavs had the Pistons in this precise situation in the conference semifinals. After a clutch win in Auburn Hills in Game Five, the Cavs had a chance to put the series in their back pocket at home in Game Six but instead lost a two-point heartbreaker. They were then blown out in Game Seven two days later, ending what had been a magical playoff run. Cleveland fans were terrified of history repeating itself in 2007.

It was a bustling Saturday night in downtown Cleveland. Appropriately, across the street from the Q, the Cleveland Indians and Detroit Tigers battled for first place in Major League Baseball's Central Division. But the real party took place in between the two arenas, where giant television screens were set up in Gateway Plaza to broadcast the Cavs' shot at history to the Mardi Gras atmosphere created on Eagle Avenue. For the first time, LeBron James's unforgettable promise made to the city of Cleveland when he was drafted by the Cavs four years earlier began to take shape. On that fateful day in the summer of 2003, he pledged to light up Cleveland like Las Vegas. Yet ironically, the first half of the most electric game in Cavs' history was defined by a power outage.

After the Cavaliers motored to a six-point lead to close the first quarter, the arena scoreboards and clocks malfunctioned prior to the start of the second, causing a twenty-one-minute delay as technicians tried to fix the problem. They couldn't, and play continued with the time remaining on the shot clock being announced over the public address system. While both teams were affected by this electronic confusion, the Cavs looked utterly lost. After a miserable 4-for-18 shooting performance in the period, their nine-point lead evaporated and the Pistons clawed back to tie the game at the intermission. At one point, James walked over to the scorer's table and made his own plea: "We've got to get it fixed." Cleveland general manager Danny Ferry pulled coach Mike Brown aside during a time out in the discombobulated second period and told him, "Don't let this be a distraction." But there was nothing Brown could do. Longtime Cleveland sports fans rolled their eyes and rubbed their temples, anticipating the next quotation mark body blow. A loss would forever etch this one as "The Clock"—joining "The Drive," "The Fumble," and "The Shot" in the lexicon of North Coast misery. The stage was set: James, who had been masterful in Game Five, missed the only two shots he attempted in the first half and was held to nine quiet points from the foul line. Often fighting through three defenders, James continued to struggle through the third period and entered the fourth with just one field goal.

Though the scoreboard and clocks were finally fixed at halftime, the Cavs continued to struggle in the third and led by just one point going into the fourth. Fans braced themselves for the fourth quarter like prairie farmers preparing for a tornado. They had, after all, seen this all too many times. With James wrapped up like a Christmas present, someone else would have to step up. And someone—perhaps the least likely candidate—did just that.

After James intercepted a Piston pass and drove the length of the floor for a layup, which became a three-point play, the fourth quarter became the Boobie Show. Daniel "Boobie" Gibson, a rookie guard who had cemented himself as a steady but not vital role player during the season, caught fire. First, with Cleveland up 70–67, he drilled a three-pointer to double the lead. James, sensing Gibson's hot hand, pulled the rookie aside during a time-out. "Get that gun out and get it locked and loaded," he told him. "Just shoot it. Don't even think about it."

With the Detroit defense still focused on James, Gibson hit another to make it 79–67, then another to push the contest out of reach at 86–71 with 6:50 remaining. There would be no quotation marks on this night. Gibson tallied the most efficient playoff performance in franchise history. Despite only taking nine shots from the floor, he scored thirty-one points, including twelve free throws and a perfect five-for-five beyond the three-point arc. James wound up with a solid twenty points, fourteen rebounds, and eight assists, but this night belonged to Boobie.

When the final buzzer sounded to conclude the 98–82 victory, James launched the basketball sixty feet into the air and soared to meet his teammates at midcourt. The first to embrace him was Zydranus Ilgauskas, who had been with the team longer than any other player. These two had been there when the Cavs began the process of turning around a sixty-five-loss team. Now that team had been crowned conference champion—and the city of Cleveland was indeed lit up like Las Vegas.

Outside the Q, the massive celebration began. The sellout crowds from both Jacobs Field and the Q spilled into the streets. Strangers embraced and car horns jubilantly blared. A franchise that had almost always taken a backseat to the Browns and Indians had become the toast of a long-suffering town—and ironically, the first in a generation to launch a championship celebration at the site of the victory. Though the Indians had reached the World Series twice in recent memory, both times they'd clinched the pennant on the road. For the first time in four decades, Cleveland was the site of a victory that propelled one of its teams to its sport's ultimate showcase. "Saturday night wasn't a distant rumbling," Bud Shaw wrote. "Saturday night brought the fireworks to your backyard."

The Cavs, who had undergone three miserable stretches of plummeting to the worst team in basketball in thirty-five years, were Eastern Conference champions. Tossing aside the memories of near misses in their two previous trips to the conference finals, they had become just the fourth team in NBA history to rally from a two-nothing deficit to win a seven-game series. And in so doing, they'd made believers out of a new generation of fans who hadn't suffered through John Elway, Earnest Byner, or Michael Jordan. On this glorious June night, all the emotional baggage of a star-crossed franchise vanished. "All Moses had to do was wave a hand and the Red Sea parted," Shaw wrote. "Moses Cleaveland had to clear a lot of brush."

James, whose moniker "The Chosen One" had been fulfilled, shrugged off the talk of jinxes and curses. "Something had to go right for Cleveland sports," he said. For one night, no one could argue. LeBron James and Company had made believers out of an entire city and started a tidal wave of momentum that would carry over to both the Indians and Browns, who combined to create a year of historic success.

"Toast to a fuzzier recollection if not a total erasure," Shaw wrote. "You earned it."

They had, and to celebrate, they lit up the city of Cleveland with a beacon of pride.

	1	2	3	4	
Pistons	21	27	18	16	=82
Cavaliers	27	21	19	31	=98

DETROIT

Player	FG-FGA	FT-FTA	Reb.	Ass.	Pts.
Prince	1–10	3–4	6	6	5
Wallace	5–14	1–1	2	2	11
Webber	5–8	3–3	6	0	13
Hamilton	10–20	8–8	4	3	29
Billups	3–7	2–3	0	1	9
Delfino	0–2	0–0	1	0	0
McDyess	2–8	3–5	6	1	7
Hunter	1–4	1–1	2	1	4
Mohammed	0–1	0–0	1	0	0
Maxiell	0–0	0–0	0	0	0
Davis	0–0	0–0	2	0	0
Murray	1–4	2–2	3	2	4
TOTAL	28–78	23–27	33	16	82

3-Point Goals: 3–14 (Hamilton 1–1, Billups 1–3, Hunter 1–4, Delfino 0–1, Murray 0–1, Prince 0–2, Wallace 0–2)

CLEVELAND

Player	FG-FGA	FT-FTA	Reb.	Ass.	Pts.
James	3–11	14–19	14	8	20
Gooden	3–9	1–2	4	0	7
Ilgauskas	5–9	1–1	12	0	11
Pavlovic	2–7	3–4	2	1	8
Hughes	3–8	1–2	3	4	9
Varejao	3–9	1–3	7	0	7
Gibson	7–9	12–15	6	2	31
Marshall	1–4	0–0	3	0	3
Da. Jones	1–6	0–0	2	4	2
Snow	0–0	0–0	0	0	0
TOTAL	28–72	33–46	53	19	98

3-Point Goals: 9–21 (Gibson 5–5, Hughes 2–4, Pavlovic 1–2, Marshall 1–3, James 0–2, Da. Jones 0–5)

Attendance: 20,562

The Miracle of Richfield

"The National Basketball Association's Eastern Conference playoff semifinals have finally run out of tomorrows."

Bill Nichols's words flowed from Thursday morning's *Plain Dealer* and further fueled an inferno of passion that had ignited for the Cavaliers—who over the past two weeks had become the most beloved group of individuals in the state of Ohio. That night, the Cavs would face the Washington Bullets, the defending conference champions, to conclude what had become an epic seven-game series. The veteran Bullets, the favorites going into the series, had gotten all they could handle and then some from the upstart Cavaliers, playing in the first playoff series in franchise history. Whatever happened in Game Seven, it would be remembered for a long time. "The two teams have played so well, somehow it seems unfair that one has to lose tonight," Hal Lebovitz wrote.

The site would be Richfield Coliseum, which, for the fourth straight game, would set an NBA attendance record. "Anyone whose doctor prescribes nitroglycerine pills," Nichols wrote, "is advised to avoid the Coliseum." Appropriately, the Cavs had spent much of Wednesday's practice changing all their verbal signals to hand signals to ensure communication in what was being called the "Din of Destiny." True to form, the arena was packed two hours before tip-off, with the crowd of better than 21,000 screaming, "We want the Cavs!" The roar was audible in both locker rooms. As he was going over his team's plan of attack, Washington coach K. C. Jones had a player stand up and hold the chalkboard still because it was vibrating so much from the crowd noise. Through the maze of tunnels on the other side of the building, just before taking the floor, the Cavs players joined hands and gathered around venerable backup center Nate Thurmond who, more than anyone, symbolized the competitive turn the franchise had taken. "Let's play it cool," Thurmond told his younger teammates. "Let's play it together." Moments later, they casually jogged onto the floor and the capacity crowd roared so loud the foundation of the building literally shook.

Just after sunset on that cool spring night, the teams began what would become one of the finest games in the history of basketball. Just as they had throughout the entire series, each team matched the other, with neither leading by more than seven points. The score was tied on eight occasions and the lead changed hands sixteen times. The Cavs led by three after one quarter, but the Bullets cut the margin to one at the half, then took a two-point lead into the fourth. In an era before constant cable sports coverage, the game was not broadcast on television, but WEWS Channel 5 would periodically break into its regular programming for updates from sports anchor Gib Shanley. With the Cavs now a national story, phone calls poured in to the *Plain Dealer* offices from around the country desperately trying to find out what was happening in Richfield—from as far away as Los Angeles and Puerto Rico. Most Clevelanders followed along on the radio, where Joe Tait secured his place in the annals of Cleveland sports history, literally screaming the play-by-play over the monstrous roar of the crowd. And through much of the fourth quarter, neither the coaches nor the players could hear the buzzer or even the officials' whistles. Fans spent the final period on their feet.

After Washington crept to a four-point advantage with 8:37 remaining, the Cavs roared back. A twenty-footer by Jim Brewer, a layup by Jim Cleamons, and a reverse layup by guard Dick Snyder highlighted an 8–0 run, which put the Cavs up by four. But to no one's surprise, the Bullets came right back, tying the game at eighty-three with two minutes left. With the shot clock winding down on the ensuing possession, Snyder, playing perhaps the finest game of his career, rebounded his own miss on a twelve-footer and put it back in to put the Cavs up 85–83. With 1:31 remaining, Washington forward Elvin Hayes was sent to the line with a chance to tie the game. But reminiscent of the final moments of Game Five, Hayes missed both shots and Thurmond grabbed the rebound. Cleveland returned the favor with a turnover, and the tension inside the Coliseum had become almost unbearable.

A three-second call on the Bullets with exactly a minute left gave Cleveland back the basketball. But as had been the theme throughout the entire series, nothing came easy. Snyder drove and missed with just over thirty seconds left, and Washington forward Jimmy Jones grabbed the loose-ball rebound. Washington scurried down the floor and Phil Chenier tied the game with a fifteen-foot jumper with twenty-four seconds left. It would all come down to the Cavaliers' final possession.

After running the clock down to nine seconds and taking time, Cleamons inbounded the ball to Snyder along the sideline. Seeing he was matched with towering center Wes Unseld, Snyder thought he could beat him to the basket. With a darting move to his left, he did, but as he broke free, Chenier stepped out of the paint. With the clock ticking down to five seconds, Snyder launched a high, arching shot from six feet away which floated over Chenier's winglike arms. "It wasn't the sweetest shot, it wasn't the easiest shot," Snyder would say. "In fact, it was not an orthodox layup. I had the feeling that if I wasn't careful, I would have shot it right through the glass." Bill Fitch watched from the bench as entranced as the crowd around him. "Just the Good Lord and Dick Snyder knew what was going to happen when Snyder got the ball," he would say later. "And for a time only the Good Lord knew."

With 21,564 fans holding their breath, the basketball kissed off the backboard and through the hoop with four seconds left. The roar was deafening as the Cavs were now on the brink of utter euphoria. But the Bullets would have one last chance.

Unseld inbounded from half-court. He lobbed a pass intended for Hayes down low, but the Big E stumbled and fell. Snyder deflected the ball, which caromed into the corner. Chenier raced after it, gathered it up, and in one fluid motion, spun and launched a desperate eighteen-foot shot. It bounced off the front of the rim as the buzzer sounded, and the game was over.

What happened next became legend.

Fans erupted onto the floor, swarming the players with unbridled adoration. Not sure where to go or which player to center on, they were fueled by energetic confusion. "I have never experienced anything like that in my life," Austin Carr said years later. "It was unreal. I remember looking over my shoulder and seeing people coming at me. They were coming from everywhere. They were frantic. It was like a flood, like something happened. I got weak in my knees. The noise— I'll never forget the noise." With the floor completely covered with humanity, the players were trapped in their affection. Thurmond, the wise old man on the club, raised his arms triumphantly and began jumping up and down like a high school player who'd won his first game. Bingo Smith, who'd won Game Two with a miracle shot, wandered around the floor screaming, "I can't believe it! I can't believe it! I can't believe it!" When Snyder tried to make his escape, he found his path blocked and had to climb into the stands and work his way around to the locker room. Fans mounted the baskets and tore them to the floor.

It would go down in history as "The Miracle of Richfield," capping one of the finest strings of playoff games in NBA history. "If there ever was a greater series played in anything less than the Finals," Fitch said, "I haven't seen it." After five years of lopsided losses and wrong-way baskets, the once-hopeless Cavaliers had come of age. Much like baseball's "Miracle Mets" of 1969, the wallflower had matured into a prom queen. And along the way, they'd taken the city on an emotional ride it would never forget.

"There was a time when some thought basketball would never draw that well here," a *Plain Dealer* editorial proclaimed Friday morning. "That has changed— permanently. The Cavs are a solid basketball team. More than that, they seem to have an uncanny ability to bring forth heroes and miracles for any occasion."

Though the site of the Miracle of Richfield is now just an open field, one can still feel the presence of the ghosts of the passionate fans who participated in it. It's a place of historical significance, a spot where destiny met reality and defined a generation. And if you listen closely over the hum of passing cars and the soft song of the surrounding wildlife, you can still hear the cheers of that fateful April night echoing through the meadows of Richfield.

"The noise hasn't stopped," Lebovitz wrote that night. "These ears will ring forever."

Correct on both counts.

	1	2	3	4	
Bullets	26	21	24	14	=85
Cavaliers	29	19	21	18	=87

WASHINGTON

Player	FG-FGA	FT-FTA	Reb.	Ass.	Pts.
Hayes	9–19	3–6	11	3	21
Weatherspoon	4–6	0–2	2	1	8
Unseld	0–1	3–4	9	4	3
Bing	5–12	2–2	5	0	12
Chenier	14–21	3–3	3	1	31
Riordan	0–3	0–0	1	0	0
Jones	3–6	0–0	3	2	6
Robinson	2–3	0–0	3	0	4
TOTAL	37–71	11–17	37	11	85

CLEVELAND

Player	FG-FGA	FT-FTA	Reb.	Ass.	Pts.
Smith	4–10	2–2	2	2	10
Brewer	5–7	2–4	16	2	12
Chones	5–11	1–1	4	3	11
Snyder	10–19	3–3	5	3	23
Cleamons	6–18	2–4	3	6	14
Carr	0–5	0–0	0	0	0
Russell	3–9	5–6	7	1	11
Thurmond	2–4	0–0	7	2	4
Walker	0–0	2–2	2	0	2
TOTAL	35–83	17–22	46	19	87

Attendance: 21,564